A PATH TO DISCOVER

INDIA · SINGAPORE · MALAYSIA

Notion Press

No.8, 3rd Cross Street, CIT Colony,
Mylapore, Chennai, Tamil Nadu – 600004

First Published by Notion Press 2020
Copyright © Natesan Ramalingam Iyer 2020
All Rights Reserved.

ISBN 978-1-64899-903-1

A PATH TO DISCOVER

NATESAN RAMALINGAM IYER

INDIA • SINGAPORE • MALAYSIA

INDICACADEMY

INDIC PLEDGE

- *I celebrate our civilisational identity, continuity & legacy in thought, word and deed.*

- *I believe our indigenous thought has solutions for the global challenges of health, happiness, peace, and sustainability.*

- *I shall seek to preserve, protect and promote this heritage in doing so,*
  - *discover, nurture and harness my potential,*
  - *connect, cooperate and collaborate with fellow seekers,*
  - *be inclusive and respectful of diverse opinions.*

ABOUT INDIC ACADEMY

Indic Academy is a non-traditional 'university' for traditional knowledge. We seek to bring about a global renaissance based on Indic civilizational and indigenous thought. We are pursuing a multidimensional strategy across time, space and cause by establishing centers of excellence, transforming intellectuals and building an ecosystem.

Indic Academy is pleased to support this book.

உ

கடவுள் வாழ்த்து (PRAYERS)

பெரியாண்டவர் துணை ஓம் சாய் ராம்

ஸ்ரீ ராமஜெயம்
ஸ்ரீ ரேணுகா பரமேஸ்வரி துணை
ஸ்ரீ வேங்கடாஜலபதி துணை

ஈஸ்வரகிருபையையும், ஸ்ரீ மஹா த்ரிபுரசுந்தரி ஸமேத ஸ்ரீ சந்திர மௌலிஸ்வர ஸ்வாமி கிருபையுடன், ஸ்ரீ ஆதிசங்கர பகவத்பாதாள் பரம்பராகத மூலாம்நாய ஸர்வக்ஞபீடம் ஸ்ரீ காஞ்சி காமகோடி பீடாதிபதி ஜகத்குரு ஸ்ரீ ஸ்ரீ ஸ்ரீ சங்கராச்சார்ய ஸ்வாமிகள் பரிபூரண அனுக்ரஹத்துடன் இந்த நூலை சமர்ப்பிக்கிறேன்.

By the divine grace of Mahadeva Eshwara, with the benevolence of Sri Chandra Mouleeswara Swami together with his consort Mahadevi Tripura Sundari, and with the blessings of Sri Adi Shankaracharya and the unbroken lineage of Sri Kanchi Kamakoti Peedam Sri Sri Sri Sankarachariya Swamigal, I dedicate and humbly submit this work (book)

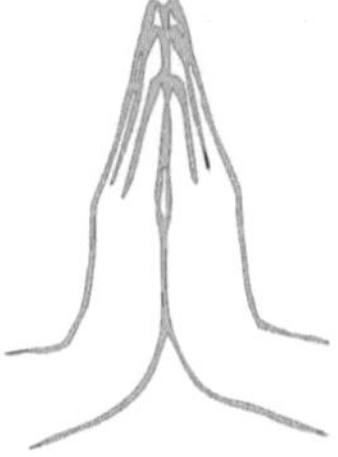

Dedicated to

- ❖ *Corona warriors dealing with Pandemic (Doctors, nurses, police-force, essential service personnel) deserving more than clapping.*

- ❖ *Services (Military) guarding the Nation.*

- ❖ *Religious Mutts, the Kendras of Knowledge inspiring faith, the bridge for all dreams & surest guide in the darkest days for a better tomorrow.*

** They are born to serve the Country, to make their fellow citizens rejoice **

CONTENTS

FOREWORD

I deem it indeed as a matter of immense pleasure and great pride to be called upon to write the foreword to the book titled "A Path to Discover "authored by Mr. Natesan Ramalingam Iyer, alias, 'Ram'.

Our friendship spans over almost 6 decades starting in June, 1964 when he joined as my junior colleague in the office I was working called the Central Designs Organisation for Tuticorin and Mangalore, Harbours Projects (CDO) under the central Ministry of Shipping and Transport and located in the premises of Madras Port. He was a Diploma Holder in Civil Engineering [Licentiate in Civil Engineering (LCE)]. I could discern the 'spark' in him while working with him which urged me to motivate him to pursue and complete AMIE qualification which was considered equivalent to engineering degree and which, I thought, was 'must' to make any further career progression by a diploma holder. Ram completed AMIE with flying colours. With this essential qualification and by dint of his three 'I's, viz., Intelligence, Industry and Integrity he went places in his career in the diversified fields of offshore oil & gas etc in engineering and managerial positions and made a mark.

Here, I recall a pleasantly strange incident. When I was Development Adviser (Ports) to Government of India, in 1998 if I remember right, I visited Bombay Port to review the progress of the ADB assisted prestigious project of Laying of submarine oil pipe lines between Pirpau and Butcher Island being executed by an international contractor. I had requested the Chief Engineer to invite the representative of the contractor also to attend the meeting. I was pleasantly surprised to see Ram, after a very long time, as the representative of the Project Management Consultant as its Area Manager! Subsequently he went many rungs up in the corporate ladder.

I learnt later that Ram is also endowed with flair for writing which propelled him to write his first book titled 'Adventures in Three Worlds' which has been published and available in online market as well.

When Ram was planning to write his second book as a sequel to his first one, the outbreak of COVID-19 has put paid to his plans for the time being at least. But the forced rest at home caused by COVID-19, has pushed him to write a book on COVID-19 itself, by way of breaking the shackles of forced rest imposed by this virus. This book contains myriads of information on COVID-19 painstakingly garnered from various sources and presented in a cogent and interesting format, as can be seen from the chapter headings, and this, I am sure, will go very well with the readers and add to their knowledge of Pandemic.

I wish Ram all the best in his future endeavours and pray the Almighty to bless him and his family with good health and happiness.

– S. GOPALAN
Retd Development Adviser (Ports)
Ministry of Shipping, Government of India

PROFILE OF S. GOPALAN

Sri. S. Gopalan is Bachelor of Engineering (B.E) in Civil Engineering graduated with First Class (Honours) from the College of Engineering, Guindy, Tamil Nadu in the year1962. His field of expertise is Ports & Harbours having served in the Ministry of Shipping, Government of India for 36 years in the areas of development and operation of ports and harbours covering the aspects of planning, design and management of ports.

Gopalan's distinguished carrier includes:

+ Served in various capacities and finally retired as the Development Adviser (Ports) to the Government of India for according technical clearance to the major port developmental projects of Major Ports. He served in the post for about 7 years.

✦ Special mention may be made of the close association from concept to commissioning stages of the Major Ports of Tuticorin, Jawaharlal Nehru and Ennore (now Kamarajar)

✦ Chaired a number of Technical Committees related to development and operation of Major Ports

✦ Technical Member of many negotiating Teams of the Government of India for financial assistance from bilateral (like Japan, Netherlands) and multilateral (like ADB and World Bank) agencies.

✦ Government nominee Trustee on the Boards of Trustees of Cochin, Paradip and Chennai

✦ Director on the Board of Directors of Dredging Corporation of India

✦ Served as Member of the Governing Body of National Institute of Port Management and Indian Institute of Port Management.

✦ Independent Director on the Board of Directors of Ennore Port Ltd (now Kamarajar Port Ltd)

✦ Mediator in the dispute between Ennore Port Ltd and its dredging contractor; also acted as one of the Members of the Expert Committee appointed for dispute resolution between Kamarajar Port Ltd and its Iron Ore Terminal Developer.

Gopalan is Fellow of the Institution of Engineers (India). He has undergone special training in ports and harbours area in Japan and UK. He has contributed number of papers relating to the subject of ports and harbours; to specifically mention he has authored a book titled "Chronicle of Ennore Port" released by the then Hon'ble Minister of Shipping. He has widely travelled on visits to many foreign ports.

Other major achievements are:

+ Deputed by Government of India to Government of Iraq as Port Expert (1979~1983) and was involved in the development of Basrah port in Iraq

+ Functioned as Chairman of the Indian Section of the Permanent International Association of Navigational Congresses (PIANC) and represented Government of India as its Chief Delegate in the main PIANC.

Gopalan is now 80 years of age, completely retired from professional life; settled in Coimbatore, Tamil Nadu with his wife, he spends his time on religious activities and reading Tamil literature. He has written a simplified form of "Ramayan Story" in a poetry form.

PREFACE

This is my second book, unintentionally compiled. My first book, "Adventures in Three Worlds", was an attempt in penning my memoire as

- ✦ World 1 - Born with shackles, struggles family went through and sacrifices made to stand-up against odds of the Society.

- ✦ World 2 - Sojourn with offshore oil & gas, life in Public Sector, and then in Private Sector, when the Industry was an Ocean of mercy, helping the whole value chain from down-hole services to CAPEX to OPEX.

- ✦ World 3 – "Post turtle" world, how difficult upstream oil & gas has become today in India for small time service providers; it is fire-fighting for them.

My wish for the second book was to write about interesting events in upstream oil & gas. It required discussing with my ex-colleagues from Ocean Engineering Division (OED) of Engineers India Ltd (EIL), all retired, and living in different parts of India and other countries. This process got aborted thanks to an outbreak of coronavirus.

This book is an out of box compilation of coronavirus events. My ambition of writing more about upstream oil & gas events has to wait for some more time.

The virus indeed emanated from Wuhan in China.

- How did this happen? Virus escaping due to some human error in a natural sequence? Or was it manufactured and the virus is completely artificial? Genetically modified?

- Did the Chinese realize in a timely manner the deadly effect of the virus, that it is highly contagious?

- Did it strike the Chinese Communists Party (CPP) that without social-distancing, the virus will turn the world into pandemic? Did they curtail their citizens traveling, especially as the emergence of virus coincided with Chinese new-year, when their citizens tend to travel abroad in bulk?

- Eventually how soon China alerted the world? Was this delayed intentionally?

- How many infected Chinese, unknowingly traveled to the rest of the world?

- Did the affected Countries react with timely measures?

- Balancing between saving lives from the virus and saving people from economic collapse?

The outbreak of the novel coronavirus has so far killed about 400,000 people and forced more than half of humanity to live under some kind of lockdown, which has crippled economies. This Tsunami has created fear and chaotic disaster, world-wide. The approximate score-card reads like this by **May 31, 2020:**

Country	Approximate Population (Million)	Infected	Fatal
USA	331	1,807,015	105,204
RUSSIA	146	405,843	4,693
SPAIN	47	286,308	27,125
BRAZIL	213	499,966	28,849
ITALY	61	232,664	33,340
FRANCE	66	151,496	28,771
GERMANY	84	183,294	8,600
IRAN	84	151,466	7,797
INDIA	**1,378**	**185,884**	**5,266**
CHINA	1,439	83,001	4,634
SINGAPORE	6	34,884	23
World	**7.8 Billion**	**6,075,786**	**369,529**

Worldwide, about 2 billion Informal workers are starving; 500 million Farmers are affected.

The European Union's 27-member bloc and many other countries including India have called for an independent evaluation of World Health Organization's (WHO's) initial response to the coronavirus pandemic "to review experience gained and lessons learned.". Any current effort to understand the origin and spread of the COVID-19 virus and a long-term strategy to deal with future pandemics must necessarily involve more than a measure of Chinese cooperation. Sustained engagement with Beijing is imperative but how far China will cooperate and come out with truth is a concern.

China has committed to provide $2 billion over two years to fight the coronavirus pandemic and the economic fallout from it, President Xi Jinping said Monday May 18, 2020 rallying around the World Health Organization even as the United States has slashed funding for the U.N. health agency and sought to undermine its credibility. As a major donor, Beijing is bound to have significant influence over WHO.

China managed to get out of coronavirus early, apparently opening the door to the rest of the world. The Covid-19 pandemic has meant countries around the world have effectively had to shut down, with many governments imposing restrictive measures on the daily lives of billions of people. If the virus is man-made, GOD knows what was their agenda? It is short term Pyrrhic victory.

To quote the Indian Prime Minister, the coronavirus crisis has taught India to "be self-sufficient and not depend on others for anything we need in our daily lives. It has made it absolutely clear that we have to depend only on ourselves for our survival". India seems to have sacrificed her economy to save lives; many countries are tending to sacrifice lives to save their economy. Ironically there was a belief that human life is cheap in India.

Countries have learnt in a hard way from the coronavirus need for self-reliant for survival. China has indeed emerged as a powerful nation through trade. China has also been accused of stealing Intellectual Property and research work, besides producing counterfeit components. Why blame China? Rest of the world is to be blamed for creating todays' China. Multi-nationals for profit have been outsourcing from China for years, never caring about their own Country's long term interests. Over the years, U.S and other countries continued prioritizing cheap labor of China. It never occurred to the politicians and multi-nationals that a balanced approach is needed for a rainy day, especially supply chain Management for the three basics - Food, Medicines and Defense. Thanks to China, what a corona reign we are going through now! Cobra effect!!

The virus brouhaha knows no borders or ethnicity. What fighter jets, missiles, and nuclear weapons could not do, Coronavirus is doing! Corona has proved that everything around us is so temporary. Things our lives revolved around…. Office, Gym, Malls, Movies, even places of worship have all gone for a toss as we are learning to live without them. It has taught us that in the end it's your own home and family that keeps you safe. The ultimate irony of life is the tiniest primitive invisible life form is now controlling the behavior of the most arrogant, powerful and evolved life form on earth. Sections of celebrities and super rich have to come out of their Narcissism. A beautiful lesson for humanity to be humble.

India is to deal with multiple issues: Corona, Migrant issues, Economic crisis, China stand-off, Pakistan terrorism, Cyclone Amphan and latest locust attack in several northern Indian States. At ground level, citizens are more concerned about Corona. The fear of the people when our country's corona count was 100 is not there when it is over 185,000 today. The answer lies in the psychological view of man. There is a philosophy called the "Kupler Rose Model". That is, when a human goes through any tragedy, natural disaster, accident, they pass through 5 stages. They are: Denial, Anger, Bargain, Depression and Acceptance. These five levels are not limited to Corona and apply to all the problems in human life. What will a wise person do? Going straight from the first level to the fifth level will set to make next steps to progress in life. The pandemic offers an opportunity to reset and restore a range of good practices that have been forsaken in a blind imitation of Western customs and behaviors, including the use of toilet paper; in simple terms, go back to "Brahminical" way of living

With globalization, no country can live on its own, unconnected. Sadly, the WHO and World Trade Organization (WTO) are not of much help.

Margaret Mead was an American cultural anthropologist and writer. She became a curator of ethnology at the American Museum of Natural History, where she published the bestselling book, Coming of Age in Samoa. Margaret Mead was once asked by a student what she considered to be the first sign of civilization in a culture. The student expected Mead to talk about clay pots, tools for hunting, grinding-stones, or religious artifacts. But no, Mead said that the first evidence of civilization was a 15,000 years old fractured femur found in an archaeological site. A femur is the longest bone in the body, linking hip to knee. In societies without the benefits of modern medicine, it takes about six weeks of rest for a fractured femur to heal. This particular bone had been broken and had healed.

Mead explained that in the animal kingdom, if you break your leg, you die. You cannot run from danger, you cannot drink or hunt for food. Wounded in this way, you are meat for your predators. No creature survives a broken leg long enough for the bone to heal. You are eaten first. A broken femur that has healed is evidence that another person has taken time to stay with the fallen, has bound up the wound, has carried the person to safety and has tended them through recovery. A healed femur indicates that someone has helped a fellow human, rather than abandoning them to save their own life.

"Helping someone else through difficulty is where civilization starts," Margaret Mead said. This is what is required today to overcome Covid-19.

Aldous Huxley's classic dystopian novel, Brave New World, was written almost 90 years ago in 1931, prior to Worldwar-2, and his insight is still highly relevant today. We are seeing in real-time the emergence of a global, technocratic super state, of which pharmaceutical companies play a critically important role and terrorism is always a lurking background threat.

In many countries especially in the U.S, in several states, folks are shouting against lockdown; is this to full-fill their want (without concern for safety of others) or is it the unemployment, poverty and hunger that are wanting them to hit the streets?

What the world is going through today is similar to Holocaust in Worldwar-2. To come out of coronavirus, one should read the story of Holocaust survivor

Eddie Jaku. During concentration camp days, a Nurse declared him as 65% dead and 35 % alive. Eddie Jaku, turned 100 in April 2020. His words:

- ✦ Please don't walk in front of me, I may not be able to follow

- ✦ Please don't walk behind me, I may not be able to lead

- ✦ Just walk besides me and be my friend.

The way the world is heading, OECD, IMF, BRICS, GROUP OF 10, OPEC, G-7, GROUP OF 8, G4 NATIONS and G-20 may become irrelevant. Nations may have to align with G-2 NATIONS, viz, U.S or CHINA. Who will be G-1 in perceivable future is anybody's guess.

To differentiate between "need" and "want", the virus has given the world *a path to discover* and choose the "NEED" rather than "WANT" and 'challenge the status quo'. Issue is "I"," MINE" and "YOU" instead of "WE". There is a big difference between a human being and being human. Only a few understand it. Pain is a sign that we're alive. Problem is a sign that we're strong. Prayer is a sign that we're not alone. When fishermen can't go to the sea, they repair their nets; lockdown is a gift to repair ourselves.

There is saying as a 10th Apple effect – the law of diminishing marginal utility; it is actually law of diminishing gratitude, in our words taking things for granted. It is lack of appreciation of gifts of life. When the dust settles down and life comes to normal, it is prudent to remember and return the gratitude to the "Front line workers" who dealt with Pandemic (Doctors, nurses, policemen, essential service personnel).

I don't claim ownership of this compilation; I'm thankful to Shiv Anand and Mahasenan former colleagues from Ocean Engineering Division of Engineers India Ltd for providing valuable inputs. The details on virus are collection from various news items and Social Media. It is well known that Social Media is not immune to fake news. To quote Mark Twain in a modified form, "If you don't log on to Social media, you are uninformed; If you do connect to Social media, you are misinformed. Readers need to keep this in their mind. Hopefully, this booklet may help the future generations to understand that coronavirus taught the world values of life and human excellence that depend on development of culture. Hopefully, Governments and People will elevate their minds to reach this stage.

– Natesan Ramalingam Iyer (RAM)

CORONA CURE POEM

Right now a virus is taking over the earth,
Attacking cities from New York to Perth !

This virus is known as corona,
It starts with fever and pneumonia.

China first had the virus now their cases are decreasing,
As for the U.S the cases are rapidly increasing.

We have to wear a mask when we go out to shop or run,
We must stay 6 feet apart from everyone.

Many countries have gone into lockdown,
Closing businesses in everytown.

There are quarantined migrant workers everywhere,
For them we must show our compassion and also our
care

We must thank doctors and nurses for putting in their time,

Not appreciating their work would be a crime.

Look on the bright side mother earth is doing well,

It deserves to - for it's gone through hell.

Unfortunately many people are dying,

Plus most have lost money hence are crying.

We have to keep calm and learn to endure,

I'm positive we will come up with a cure.

~ Shloka Satish (*)

(*) Shloka Satish, aged 12, is the Author's youngest granddaughter based in Singapore. She has developed a passion for writing poems since the age of eight, and her talent to do has greatly been appreciated by her school. Besides poetry, Shloka is also interested in Music; she successfully completed grade 5 Singing exam in the Associated Board of the Royal Schools of Music (ABRSM), U.K. She is now aiming to complete the next level while pursuing her interest in poetry.

GLOBALIZATION

As per Merriam-Webster dictionary, "Globalization" is the development of an increasingly integrated global economy marked especially by free trade, free flow of capital, and the tapping of cheaper foreign labor markets.

On paper Globalization aims to benefit individual economies around the world by making markets more efficient, increasing competition, limiting military conflicts, and spreading wealth more equally.

The Milken Institute's "Globalization of the World Economy" report of 2003 highlighted many of the benefits associated with globalization while outlining some of the associated risks that governments and investors should consider, and the principles of this report remain relevant.

Some of the benefits of globalization supposed to bring are:

✦ Foreign Direct Investment: Foreign direct investment (FDI) tends to increase at a much greater rate than the growth in world trade, helping boost technology transfer, industrial restructuring, and the growth of global companies.

+ Technological Innovation: Increased competition from globalization helps stimulate new technology development, particularly with the growth in FDI, which helps improve economic output by making processes more efficient.

+ Economies of Scale: Globalization enables large companies to realize economies of scale that reduce costs and prices, which in turn supports further economic growth. However, this can hurt many small businesses attempting to compete domestically.

Risks of globalization include:

+ **Interdependence:** Interdependence between nations can cause regional or global instabilities if local economic fluctuations end up impacting a large number of countries relying on them.

+ National Sovereignty: Some see the rise of nation-states, multinational or global firms, and other international organizations as a threat to sovereignty. Ultimately, this could cause some leaders to become nationalistic or xenophobic.

+ Equity Distribution: The benefits of globalization can be unfairly skewed towards rich nations or individuals, creating greater economic inequalities.

Writing in the quarterly Milken Institute Review in late 2017, Dani Rodrik, author of "Straight Talk on Trade: Ideas for a Sane World Economy," argued that a rebalancing of globalization is necessary to restore more voice to labor and its needs for job and income stability while focusing attention globally on where the biggest economic gains can be made. One of the balancing acts is the imposition of Tariffs and Other Forms of Protectionism.

"Globalization" is a new word for *"Trading"*. History shows that "trade" was used as a catalyst to take over or rule other Countries. Seeds of British rule of India sewed through East India Company (EIC). The East India Company was an English company formed for the exploitation of trade with East and Southeast Asia and India. Incorporated by royal charter on December 31, 1600, it was started as a monopolistic trading body so that England could participate in the East Indian spice trade. The Company was an English and later British joint-stock company.

EIC is just not one example of a trading route to take over Countries; history shows, the same trading strategy was used by the Dutch (In Indonesia), French (In India & Canada), Portugal (In India) and Spanish (In South America).

China's Belt and Road Initiative (BRI) is an ambitious "Trade program" to connect Asia with Africa and Europe via land and maritime networks along six corridors; aim? Improving regional integration, stimulating economic growth and increasing trade *(For whom, obviously China?)*

The name was coined in 2013 by China's President Xi Jinping, who drew inspiration from the concept of the Silk Road established during the Han Dynasty 2,000 years ago – an ancient network of trade routes that connected China to the Mediterranean via Eurasia for centuries. The BRI has also been referred to in the past as 'One Belt One Road'.

The BRI comprises a Silk Road Economic Belt – a trans-continental passage that links China with South-east Asia, South Asia, Central Asia, Russia and Europe by land – and a 21st century Maritime Silk Road, a sea route connecting China's coastal regions with South east and South Asia, the South Pacific, the Middle East and Eastern Africa, all the way to Europe.

The initiative defines five major priorities:

- policy coordination;
- infrastructure connectivity;
- unimpeded trade;
- financial integration and
- connecting people.

The program is expected to involve over US$1 trillion in investments, largely in infrastructure development for ports, roads, railways and airports, as well as power plants and telecommunications networks.

BRI's geographical scope is constantly expanding. So far it covers over 70 countries, accounting for about

65 per-cent of the world's population and around one-third of the world's Gross Domestic Product (GDP).

At the end of the day, given the pace China is moving, Globalization or Trading or Inside trading all tend to:

+ Proxy rule or puppet government, supporting China

+ Flood the markets with cheap Chinese goods

+ Kill domestic growth in Countries, make them depend on products or funding from China.

When discussing Globalization, it is prudent to bring the U.S in the picture. U.S became the richest economy in the World, built over several years. Most free-world people have a liking for the U.S. With the U.S, there's a difference; a Country of equal opportunity. It's the people who build the prosperity not the government, not a party, unlike the communist regimes who do it by hook and crook. That's the secret of success of the U.S. So long as the government doesn't interfere with the free will of the people, the country will always succeed. That's the reason people (not the refugees) from all over the world flock here to the U.S - not to China, Russia or for that matter even Europe.

It is how it started in the U.S; over a period of time, Super rich biggies in the U.S started reverse engineering of Chinese Communists Party (CPP) model, I mean profit is the only motto.

MBA has ruined businesses, Wall Street mentality. They are top management running companies, with no interest in production, but just profit, margins, taking over competitors, outsource from China and similar. The theme of Globalization! How many of U.S Biggies will be ready to shift their business from China? Will they do this as an obligation to their Country and Society, beyond "profit and Wall-street Bourse" considerations?

The seed for the rise of China started way back in 1971 with Henry Kissinger's secret trip to Beijing on July 9-11, 1971. Kissinger, Nixon's National Security Advisor, flew to Beijing from Pakistan after visit to India. He developed a rapprochement between the United States and the People's Republic of China, the first official U.S. contact with that nation since the Chinese Communists had come to power. Now look at what China has done to the World! They are working to make substantial population of the world depend on them through BRI.

CHITTY CHITTY WUHAN WUHAN

Coronavirus (COVID-19) originated from Wuhan in China first reported by December 31, 2019. During Chinese new year window (end January/ early February 2020), substantial tourist movement of Chinese occurred to many countries across the globe, in addition to business travels. Apparently, there were direct flights between Wuhan and Milano in Italy catering to substantial business interests. Italy and Spain were, to start-with, worst hit by this virus outside China. U.S, rest of Europe and Russia are not lagging behind; in fact, the U.S tops World in coronavirus cases, over taking Italy and Spain.

Food habits of Chinese are well known, they will eat anything that is moving; added tit-bit on Chinese is:

"In case one has missed it, Boston CBS reported on January 28, 2020, arrested by Federal Agents of Dr. Charles Lieber, chair of Harvard University's Department of Chemistry and Chemical Biology, with lying to the Department of Defense about secret monthly payments of $50,000.00 paid by

China and receipt of millions more to help set up a chemical/biological "Research" laboratory in China. Also arrested were two Chinese "Students" working as research assistants, one of whom was actually a lieutenant in the Chinese Army, the other captured at Logan Airport as he tried to catch a flight to China - smuggling 21 vials of "Sensitive Biological Samples" according to the FBI.

The research lab the good professor had helped set up? It's located at the Wuhan University of Technology. Wuhan China is ground zero to the potential global pandemic known as the "Coronavirus" which is both spreading rapidly and killing people.

This is International spy novel stuff happening in real life - and it has barely made the news."

The World Health Organization referred to it as a pandemic on March 11, 2020.

An episode of the 2003 U.S television show Dead Zone has left people wondering if Hollywood had predicted the coronavirus outbreak years before we even had the notion of the deadly pandemic turning our lives upside down. In the episode titled "Plague" Johnny Smith, a retired school teacher gets a vision of a group of children becoming extremely ill after they are infected with a mysterious virus. He informs the town sheriff about what he saw and asks him to quarantine the school building as the children start to get sick. The episode shows that the local health inspector while trying to figure out where the virus came from talks about China as the source and has people who have recently travelled as one of the ways virus could have been transmitted. It also talks about how the US-based Centers for Disease Control and Prevention (CDC) is said to take months to figure out a cure or where it originated from. The episode also emphasis on the immediate lockdown. There is also a discussion about wearing masks!

An American film that was shown in 2011 speaks of a Corona like virus that began to spread to the rest of the world! The strangest thing is that at the end of the movie it turns out that the cause of infection is the bat, which is the same reason that the disease is currently spread!!The name of the film is, "Contagion" and it stars Matt Damon, Jude Law, Gwyneth Paltrow and Kate Winslet. Yes, it was prophetic.

There is also a book "End of days": Predictions and Prophecies about the End of the World by Sylvia Browne with Lindsay Harrison. This book was first published in 2008. The photo excerpts from the book are going viral on social media and people are spooked enough as it is. This book has a passage that says. "In around 2020, severe pneumonia-like illness will spread across the globe, attacking the lungs and bronchial tubes and resisting all known treatments. Almost more baffling than the treatment itself will be the fact that it will suddenly vanish as quickly as it arrived, attack again in ten years later, and then disappearing completely."

Coronavirus is indeed dangerous, given its multiplying effect world-wide. Apart from this:

1. Is this an economic solution for China at the expense of the rest of the World?

2. Is the purpose of the media campaign to settle the trade war between China and America

3. To reduce financial markets - to prepare the stage of financial markets for mergers and acquisitions

As the World is infected with Coronavirus, a new theory is emerging, mentioning that the virus is an economic solution created by Chinese. The Chinese president was at Wuhan Hospital without a muzzle. China officially announces victory over the Coronavirus. China has miraculously "recovered" with almost no more cases of coronavirus. Rest of the world is now beginning to feel the effects and panic about the disease. On the economic front, the effect of this virus is deadly, many global markets closing index dropping by as much as 20 ~ 30 %.

How far the theory that the virus is an economic solution created by Chinese is true, we will never know. However, it is a fact that the virus first emanated from Wuhan in China.

Dany Shoham, a former Israeli military intelligence officer who has studied Chinese biological warfare, said the institute is linked to Beijing's covert bio-weapons program. "Certain laboratories in the institute have probably been engaged, in terms of research and development, in Chinese [biological weapons], at least collaterally, yet not as a principal facility of the Chinese BW alignment," Mr. Shoham told The Washington Times.

Work on biological weapons is conducted as part of dual civilian-military research and is "definitely covert," he said in an email. Mr. Shoham holds a doctorate in medical microbiology. From 1970 to 1991, he was a senior analyst with Israeli military intelligence for biological and chemical warfare in the Middle East and worldwide. He held the rank of lieutenant colonel.

Gao Fu, director of the Chinese Center for Disease Control and Prevention, told state-controlled media that initial signs indicated the virus originated from wild animals sold at a seafood market in Wuhan.

China has denied having any offensive biological weapons, but a State Department report last year revealed suspicions of covert biological warfare work.

China deployed military forces to Wuhan to halt all travel out of the city of 11 million people in an effort to contain the outbreak of the virus, which causes pneumonia like symptoms.

The Wuhan institute has studied coronaviruses including the strain that causes severe acute respiratory syndrome (SARS), H5N1 influenza virus, Japanese encephalitis and dengue. Researchers at the institute also have studied the germ that causes anthrax, a biological agent once developed in Russia. "Coronaviruses [particularly SARS] have been studied in the institute and are probably held therein," Mr. Shoham said. "SARS is included within the Chinese BW program, at large, and is dealt with in several pertinent facilities."

Biological weapons convention: Mr. Shoham, is now with the Begin-Sadat Center for Strategic Studies at Bar Ilan University in Israel. In one of the articles in the journal Institute for Defense Studies and Analyses, Mr. Shoham said the Wuhan institute was one of four Chinese laboratories engaged in some aspects of biological weapons development.

China declared a second facility, the Wuhan Institute of Biological Products, as one of eight biological warfare research facilities covered by the Biological Weapons Convention, which China joined in 1985. The Wuhan Institute of Biological Products is a civilian facility but is linked to the Chinese defense establishment. Mr. Shoham said it is thought to be involved in the Chinese Biological Weapons Convention program. China's vaccine against SARS is probably produced there. "This means the SARS virus is held and propagated there, but it is not a new coronavirus unless the wild type has been modified, which is not known and cannot be speculated at the moment," he said.

The annual State Department report on arms treaty compliance stated last year that China engaged in activities that could support biological warfare. "Information indicates that the People's Republic of China engaged during the reporting period in biological activities with potential dual-use applications, which raises concerns regarding its compliance with the BWC," said the report, adding that the United States suspects China failed to eliminate its biological warfare program as required by the treaty.

"The United States has compliance concerns with respect to Chinese military medical institutions' toxin research and development because of the potential dual-use applications and their potential as a biological threat," the report said. The biosafety lab is about 20 miles from the Hunan Seafood Market, which reports from China say may have been the origin point of the virus.

The coronavirus outbreak has brought the world to a halt both physically and economically. COVID-19 outbreak has caused global panic.

With global media, speculations about the communist government of China trying to 'cover-up' the outbreak and hide the official figures are rife. Did the Chinese deceive the world with the Coronavirus? And they saved their economy?! This is what the Americans and Europeans think, after they sold their shares in high-value-added technology companies for a minimal price to the Chinese government. According to them, the Chinese leadership used an "economic tactic" that made everyone swallow the bait easily, before they asserted that China did not resort to implementing a high political strategy to get rid of European investors, in support of China's economy, which would bypass the US economy with this step!

And because it teaches the science of certainty that Europeans and Americans are looking for excuses to slow and bankrupt the Chinese economy, China has sacrificed some hundreds of its citizens, instead of sacrificing entire country! Through this tactic, China succeeded in "deceiving all", as it reaped about $ 20 billion in two days, and the Chinese president succeeded in deceiving the European Union and the United States of America in the eyes of the world, and played an economic game of a tactical nature, which was unthinkable!

Before the Coronavirus, most of the stocks and stakes in investment projects at "Technology and Chemicals" production plants were owned by European and American investors! This means that more than half of the profits from the light and heavy technological and chemical industries went to the hands of foreign investors, not to the Chinese treasury, which led to a decline in the Chinese currency, the yuan and the Chinese central bank could not do something against the continuous fall of the yuan! There was even widespread news that China was unable to purchase masks to prevent the spread of the deadly virus. These rumors and the Chinese President's statements that he is "not ready to save the country from the virus" have led to a sharp drop in the purchase prices of shares of technology companies in China, and the empires of "foreign" investors have raced to offer investment shares for sale at very low prices, and with attractive offers, "never seen before" in history! The Chinese government waited for foreign share prices to reach their "almost free" minimums, and then issued an order to purchase them. And bought the shares of Americans and Europeans! And when European and American investment financiers realized that they had been deceived, it was too late, as the shares were in the hands of the Chinese government, which in this process nationalized most of the foreign companies erected on its soil in a near-free manner, without causing a political crisis or a single shot!

The same sources confirmed and pointed out that "Corona" is a "real" virus, but it is not a terrible danger that has been promoted across the world! China began to take out the anti-virus vaccine, this vaccine that it had owned from the beginning on the shelves of refrigerators after it had achieved its goal!

China, creator of the pandemic, has miraculously "recovered", has almost no more cases of coronavirus. The world is now beginning to feel the effects and panic about the disease. Who recovered first?? China itself! It seems to be that this virus was a move by the Chinese government in response to the loss of the trade war with the United States. The goal: to throw the world into recession!!! Is the scenario not clear? They are already growing! China bought almost everything it devalued on the stock exchanges around the world... with that the Chinese became owners of the global companies that are in China and without the money leaving China.

Wuhan to Shanghai = 839 km

Wuhan to Beijing = 1152 km

Milan from Wuhan = 15000 km

Wuhan to New York = 15000 km

Wuhan to Etli = 8695 km

Wuhan to India = 3695 km

Wuhan to Iran = 5667 km

Corona has no significant effect in nearby Beijing / Shanghai areas, but deaths in U.S, Italy, Iran, European countries, ruining the world economy. All business areas of China are safe, something is fishy?

1. Where the whole world is being affected by this, why did it not spread widely anywhere in China except Wuhan? How did China's capital remain untouched by this?

2. Why did China hide from the whole world about the virus?

3. Why destroy the initial sample of Corona?

4. Why did the doctor and the journalist who brought it up be silenced? Has the journalist been exterminated?

5. When other countries of the world asked to share information, why did they not share the information? Why refuse

6. Why was the Director of WHO used to hide the spread of corona from human to human? WHO Director was doing what he did in "Beijing (China)" in January? (fixing the plan?)

7. "There is no need to issue any guideline for any international flight, as it does not spread from human to human" WHO kept doing this tweet till January 11, 2020. Why? Today it has been proved that corona spreads from human to human so why did the WHO lie?

8. Why were about 5 million people sent from Wuhan "to different parts of the world" without medical examination?

9. There was a minor case in Italy till 6 February. Suddenly a slogan 'We are Chinese, not a virus, embrace us.' Why did they come to embrace the people of Italy with placards in the world's tourist destination known as 'City of Love' (Milano)

Prominent Virologist Xiangguo Qiu, her colleague husband Keding Cheng and their Chinese were students thrown out of Canada's National Microbiology Lab at Winnipeg. Yanqing Ye, 29, a Chinese national, was charged in an indictment today with one count each of visa fraud, making false statements, acting as an agent of a foreign government and conspiracy. He is currently in China.

Zaosong Zheng, 30, a Chinese national, was arrested on Dec. 10, 2019, at Boston's Logan International Airport and charged by criminal complaint with attempting to smuggle 21 vials of biological research to China. On Jan. 21, 2020, Zheng was indicted on one count of smuggling goods from the United States and one count of making false, fictitious or fraudulent statements. He has been detained since Dec. 30, 2019

Wuhan Institute of Virology has more than 1500 virus strains and was possibly working on a Biological Weapon of mass destruction illegally!! Maybe one of the scientists got infected while engineering these viruses. The same virus got spread through the Meat Market some 300 metres away from the institute.

Some 60,000 people moved out from The Transit Hub Wuhan to different parts of the world in January 2020 which could have been avoided !! This migration resulted in the spread of the virus worldwide !!

More than 20 Million Cellphones in China are reported to have gone dead in the past 2 months!! The actual no of death in China has been kept under wraps as it can go to millions!! Crematoriums worked 24 X 7 to dispose of the dead apart from burials in Hubei

Province. Many Old sick people were killed / burnt to make way for new patients in hospitals!!

Seeing the economy going down the president of China Xi Jinping has asked for workers to restart work stating that the virus has been contained with no new infections which is doubtful !! This was further supported by media world-wide.

The Chinese media is state controlled and filters all reports going out as per the ruling Communist Party's agenda. There have been fresh cases of infection and contamination in Beijing & Shanghai.

WHO Director General Tedros Adhanom worked as the Health Minister of Ethiopia till 2012 and has affiliations with Tigrayans people liberation front which is a leftist party. With help from China he was elected as DG in WHO. Was he paying back the favour by going soft in on China for its lack in of controlling the virus & informing the world about the epidemic

China has begun an all-out war using Social media and Mainstream media as well buying many media reporters' houses, politicians to change the narrative by blaming the US rather than accepting it's fault!!

Mike Pompeo spoke to reporters after the G7 leaders held a meeting by videoconference.

US Secretary of State Mike Pompeo said Group of Seven foreign ministers agreed with him in talks that

China was waging a "disinformation" campaign about the coronavirus pandemic.

The top diplomats from the major industrialized nations held a previously scheduled meeting by videoconference, with the United States scrapping a meeting in Pittsburgh as the contagion fears restrict international travel.

Pompeo, who has heavily criticized Beijing over what he calls the "Wuhan virus," said he was united with other ministers - from Britain, Canada, France, Germany, Italy and Japan.

"Every one of the nations that were at that meeting this morning was deeply aware of the disinformation campaign that the Chinese Communist Party is engaged in to try and deflect from what has really taken place," Pompeo told reporters after the talks.

Pompeo said that China "has been and continues to be engaged in" a campaign on social media that has included conspiracy theories that the United States was behind the virus, which was first detected in the Chinese metropolis of Wuhan. "This is crazy talk," Pompeo said.

The G7 talks came a day before a virtual summit of leaders of the Group of 20 major economies, which include the United States and China.

Beijing has appeared to bring the virus under control and has stepped up aid by delivering masks and other supplies around the world - including to US allies such as Italy.

China is "now making small sales of products around the world and claiming that they are now the white hat in what has taken place," Pompeo said. But he said the United States sought cooperation.

"We desperately want to work with every country around the world. This is a global pandemic," he said. "The United States wants to work with every country including China to figure out how to resolve to keep as many people alive - as many people as healthy - and then to restore our economies that have been decimated by the Wuhan virus." (AFP)

The meeting from SAARC to G-20, India has emerged as a world leader in times of crisis, when Italy, Germany, Spain, France, Britain, America are failing to deal with Corona effectively.

Interesting about a Book by Chinese colonels Qiao Liang and Wang Xiangsui, from 1999, "Unrestricted Warfare: China's master plan to destroy America", on Amazon.

China is accelerating New Infrastructure investment $3.4 Trillion as part of stimulus measures to help stabilize growth and employment, help consumption, and improve the overall quality of life, one of the pet projects being Belt & Road Initiative (BRI). This is all in Technology infrastructure - 5G et al. That will put them way ahead.

About China's generosity in this time of crisis, they sent $300 million worth of equipment and materials (masks) etc to Spain. Apparently 70% of the items shipped were substandard and Spain has returned the lot.

Given Wuhan emanated virus, it appears that China has won the 3rd World War without firing a missile; no Country could handle it yet.

The fact that the Chinese Government tried to suppress the attempts of their whistleblowers who were warning the public of the pandemic, is sad. While the rumours of the Chinese cover-up are unsubstantiated, once can only think about the popular proverb, 'there's no smoke, without fire'.

Is Coronavirus A Bioweapon? According to an ET Prime report, a group of Chinese scientists in Canada were accused of spying and were stripped of their access to Canada's National Microbiology Lab (NML) which is known to work on some of the most deadly pathogens.

The alleged 'policy breach', highlighted the bioweapon program of other countries including China. Dr Francis Boyle, the creator of Bioweapons Act, also claims that 'the coronavirus is an offensive biological warfare weapon with DNA-genetic engineering'. Again, the claims about coronavirus being a biological weapon are unsubstantiated.

Scientists haven't been able to determine the origin of COVID-19 but speculations are rife that the virus originated in the seafood market. This was substantiated by reports from Chinese health authorities and the World Health Organization which said that "most" cases had links to the seafood market, which was closed on January 01, 2020.

Skeptics on the online forums, however, have been sharing suspicions that the virus could have originated from Wuhan, Institute of Virology, which houses China's only level- four biosafety laboratory (the highest-level classification of labs that study the deadliest viruses). The first prominent personality to come out publicly and support the theory was the US senator Tom Cotton who appeared on Fox News to allege that the virus could indeed have originated from the lab. Several netizens have also been alleging that this was an attempt to control the Chinese population. However, the claims are unsubstantiated.

If indeed the virus is created by *someone or some country,* the World should rally and fix responsibility on the Creator, the culprit. We can take a cue from the Deepwater Horizon oil spill (also referred to as the BP oil spill, oil leak, or oil disaster; the Gulf of Mexico oil spill; and the Macondo blowout). This is an industrial disaster that began on April 20, 2010, in the Gulf of Mexico on the BP-operated Macondo Prospect, considered to be the largest marine oil spill in the history of the petroleum industry and estimated to be 8% to 31% larger in volume than the previously largest, the Ixtoc I oil spill, also in the Gulf of Mexico. The U.S. federal government estimated the total discharge at 4.9 million barrels (210 million US gal; 780,000 m3). The Deepwater Horizon oil spill is regarded as one of the largest environmental disasters in American history. In September 2014, a U.S. District Court judge ruled that BP was primarily responsible for the oil spill because of its gross negligence and reckless conduct. In July 2015, BP agreed to **pay $18.7 billion in fines**, the largest corporate settlement in United States history.

It is reported that the International Council of Jurists (ICJ) and All India Bar Association (AIBA) have filed a complaint in the United Nations Human Rights Council seeking unspecified amounts as reparations from China over the global spread of coronavirus. The petition filed accused China of inaction and negligence on spreading the virus worldwide and alleged that the country had violated International Health Regulations (IHR), and International Human Rights and as also International Humanitarian Laws and UDHR clauses.

A similar legal suit has also been filed in the US against Chinese authorities claiming that the coronavirus outbreak is a result of biological weapons. The lawsuit is against the Chinese army, the Wuhan Institute of Virology, Director of Wuhan Institute of Virology Shi Zhengli and Chinese army's Major

General Chen Wei. The lawsuit (Reported as $20 trillion) accuses China of aiding and abetting death, provision of material support to terrorists, conspiracy to cause injury and death of US citizens, negligence, wrongful death, and assault and battery. The petition was filed by American lawyer Larry Klayman and his advocacy group Freedom Watch along with Texas company Buzz Photos. They had also alleged that the virus was released from the Wuhan Virology Institute. In essence, a disease that was spread by the folks as they flew around the globe will now kill millions of the poor.

German magazine Bild editor has accused China of being the cause of the Covid-19 outbreak and demanding massive reparations. "What China owes us," a provocative article in German tabloid Bild published on 15 April, put a price tag of nearly □150 billion for damages inflicted on the country by Covid-19 pandemic. China responded in anger in an open letter to Bild editor Julian Reichelt pointing out that China warned the world early of the dangers of the virus, while rejecting any obligation to pay damages. It also reproached Bild "nationalism, prejudice, and hostility against China."

Reichelt countered with another open letter, saying that Chinese President Xi Jinping "rules by surveillance," which is a "denial of freedom," charging that Beijing didn't respond to western requests after it discovered the virus in Wuhan. It concluded that

"...China is known as a surveillance state that infected the world with a deadly disease. That is your political legacy."

These avalanches of suits have no effect on China. Unfortunately, legality is a matter of *Power*, not *Justice*.

A powerful documentary is circulating on the Chinese Communist Party CCP the C-19 virus & tracking down the origin at the Wuhan Institute.

LINK:

https://www.youtube.com/watch?v=3bXWGxhd7ic & feature=youtu.be

- ✦ December 30, 2019 China announced unknown Pneumonia cases linked to the Wuhan seafood market,

- ✦ January 24, 2020 The lancet (world's leading independent general medical journal) challenged this conclusion repeatedly & said the latest cases had no links to the Wuhan seafood market

- ✦ January 10, 2020 the Chinese released the genome sequence which showed a relationship with bats from Zhoushan east china, it is not possible that the S protein can be a natural mutation. S proteins or Spike proteins unlock the ACE2 receptors in the human respiratory system.

- ✦ anuary 03, 2020 Chinese communist party censored all information on the Virus

✦ In 2015 the Wuhan institute Dr Shi Zhengli published a paper stating that 26 viruses found in bats encoding the SHCO14 spike found in a wild type backbone can effectively use multiple orthologs of the SARS receptor for human angiotensin converting enzyme II ACE2 receptors in human airways.

✦ Why would the Chinese create a virus link between a HIV GP14 & a human ACE2 receptor in the lungs, surely this can only be for unethical activity?

✦ 2019 Wuhan Institute Dr Shi Zhengli confirms the C-19 virus uses the same cell entry through the ACE2 receptor as SARS.

✦ January 02, 2020 Wuhan Institute prohibits disclosure of information to any source.

✦ January 21, 2020 US provide REDESIVIR to China to help treat Chinese patients - then applied for a patent by the Wuhan institute.

✦ February 03, 2020 Dr Wu blows the whistle on Dr Shi Zhengli (the C-19 expert) haphazard laboratory management.

✦ French money built the Wuhan Institute

President Donald Trump said he intends to bill China for a 'substantial' amount for damages caused by the coronavirus. During a press conference at the White House on Monday April 27, Trump made a threat to

China after being asked whether he was considering seeking money from Beijing for its response to the pandemic. He has again repeated this in a press briefing on April 30, 2020:

+ World Health Organization (WHO) is like PR agency for China

+ Proof links China lab to virus

In the six days after top Chinese officials secretly determined they likely were facing a pandemic from a new coronavirus, the city of Wuhan at the epicenter of the disease hosted a mass banquet for tens of thousands of people, and millions began traveling through for Lunar New Year celebrations.

President Xi Jinping warned the public on the seventh day, Jan. 20. But by that time, more than 3,000 people had been infected during almost a week of public silence, according to internal documents obtained by The Associated Press and expert estimates based on retrospective infection data.

Six days.

That delay from Jan. 14 to Jan. 20 was neither the first mistake made by Chinese officials at all levels in confronting the outbreak nor the longest lag, as governments around the world have dragged their feet for weeks and even months in addressing the virus. But the delay by the first country to face the new coronavirus came at a critical time: the beginning of the outbreak. China's attempt to walk a line between alerting the public and avoiding panic set the stage for a pandemic that has infected almost 4.8 million people and taken more than 315,000+ lives.

"This is tremendous," said Zuo-Feng Zhang, an epidemiologist at the University of California, Los Angeles. "If they took action six days earlier, there would have been much fewer patients and medical facilities would have been sufficient.

Dr. Anthony Fauci, the top infectious diseases expert on the White House coronavirus task force, appeared on MSNBC Sunday April 12, 2020 evening to speak about when the administration concluded that coronavirus was a threat and how Chinese "misinformation" about whether the virus could spread person-to-person delayed the U.S. response. Fauci said he decided it was a danger to America after "it was clear that some of the misinformation we initially got from China -- their first cases were reported at the very end of December... They said it was something like 24 cases in this 'wet market' where these exotic animals are sold". By the time we got that information and we started getting cases here, it was, 'well, it's not efficiently spread from human-to-human.' But as soon as it became clear that there was community spread, which means that it isn't just a travel-related case, that there are cases that are in the community under the radar screen, then it became clear that we were in real trouble," Fauci said

There is call to bring supply lines back to the United States; this will have bipartisan resonance as the pandemic has focused glaring attention on America's dependence on China for drugs and medical equipment Many countries have this problem of dependence on China

No country is yet to sue China for damages or made a move to go to International Court of Justice (ICJ) against China. Will any Country receive these impairment costs from China? Answer is no; China is too powerful and will fast track BRI. There are lots of Countries who will favor China, thanks to their leadership compromising their countries for personal and short term political gains. Hypothetically, any amount of compensation can't bring dead to life again.

China surprised the world on May 01, 2020 that they have decided to cancel the dollar peg in the stock exchange transactions and decided to officially link the Chinese yuan instead of the dollar, and this is a bold and important step in China's economic history. This means that the dollar has become non-existent in Chinese trading and the US dollar will fall strongly against the Chinese yuan and may affect it in global markets. And all the global markets were stunned by the decision. The news was discussed today on the BBC World English afternoon program. It is an economic war that could lead the world to a devastating war that cannot be neglected if America acts foolishly in the face of this decision! China 2021 will lead the world. This is China's old dream and what it planned to achieve for decades or more.

China plans a separate digital currency e-RMB, to take on fights with US$

https://amp.theguardian.com/world/2020/apr/28/china-starts-major-trial-of-state-run-digital-currency

e-RMB, which is set to be the first digital currency operated by a major economy. A sovereign digital currency provides a functional alternative to the dollar settlement system and blunts the impact of any sanctions or threats of exclusion both at a country and company level," last week's China Daily report said. Some government employees and public servants are to receive their salaries in the digital currency from May.

A decline in cash usage is expected to continue amid the growing popularity of digital payment platforms and as people avoid physical contact during the coronavirus pandemic. It may also facilitate integration into globally traded currency markets with a reduced risk of politically inspired disruption

The lab -- the Wuhan National Biosafety Laboratory (Level 4) of the Chinese Academy of Sciences -- works with and studies the world's most dangerous pathogens such as Severe Acute Respiratory

Syndrome (SARS), and Ebola. However, scientists had warned in 2017 that a dangerous virus could escape the lab. As more and more investigations are taking place it has been revealed that the U.S. government gave a $3.7 million grant to Wuhan lab at the center of coronavirus leak scrutiny that was performing experiments on bats from the caves where the disease is believed to have originated. The Wuhan Institute of Virology, the most advanced laboratory of its type on the Chinese mainland, is based twenty miles from the now infamous wildlife market that was thought to be the location of the original transfer of the virus from animals to humans.

Why did the U.S. government give $3.7 million grant to Wuhan lab?

- Was it a real philanthropist goodwill action for R&D and they had great confidence in this lab?

- Or was the U.S concerned about carrying out such R&D experiments in the U.S as a high risk exercise; and better to shift this activity to China; if there is leak or infection, it would be to the Chinese locally in Wuhan

We will never know.

As of now, is there clear evidence of conspiracy theory on Chinese? Answer is NO. The broad scientific consensus holds that SARS-CoV-2, the official name of the coronavirus, originated in bats. However, there is no factual evidence corroborating the information recently circulating in the United States press that establishes a link between the origins of COVID-19 and the work of the P4 laboratory of Wuhan, China. Having said this, is the free world trusting China? Answer is no. There is concern that with China being ahead of the rest of the world on 5G, they are capable of covering themselves. Also history shows that China can't be trusted:

+ Sino – India war of 1962. China retained actual control of the Aksai Chin region off Himalayan border.

+ The annexation of Tibet in 1959

+ Bullying Taiwan, in the name of "one China policy"

+ Claim by China over India's State of Arunachal Pradesh

+ China has a history of infecting the world

+ They have a history of running substandard laboratories and supplying substandard products.

+ Recent occupation of disputed territory in south china sea, while the world was watching as mute spectator

+ China trying to attract world's attention towards Tibetan side of Mt Everest? Summit of Mount Everest sits exactly on the border between Nepal and Tibet. Recently, China installed 5G network on the Tibetan side of Everest. The world was taken by surprise when the official website of China Global Television Network (CGTN) has published a tweet with pictures of Mount Everest. The tweet states "An extraordinary sun halo was spotted Friday in the skies over Mount #Qomolangma, also known as Mount Everest, the world's highest peak located in China's Tibet Autonomous Region".

+ Mr. Pandemic shadow boxing instigating Nepal to make noise against India on border issues.

+ China bullying India with military activities near Ladakh, Line of Actual Control (LOC).

+ China is set to introduce a new security law for Hong Kong, seen strengthening hold over city, effectively circumventing the Hong Kong government, undercutting the relative autonomy granted to the territory.

Going by a popular proverb, 'there's no smoke, without fire', it is prudent to mention two interesting stories. One is an article purported to be written by Giacomino Nicolazzo; his story runs like this:

QUOTE

ITALY DESTROYED - Who could have seen this in Italy, everything was hushed up!

ITALY'S RECIPE FOR DISASTER

Published March 24, 2020 | By Giacomino Nicolazzo

Giacomino Nicolazzo is one of Italy's most beloved writers. Born and raised in Central Pennsylvania USA, he lives in a small village in Lombardy where he writes his books. Montecalvo, Lombardy, Italy.

As I sit here in my involuntary isolation, it was just reported that overnight 743 more people died and 5.249 new cases have been reported. This brings the total cases of infection to 69,176 and the body count to 6,820. We take relief in knowing that 8,326 people have recovered so far. (Numbers as of March 24, 2020 8:30pm in Italy.

Most towns here in Italy, from the upper reaches of the Alps to the ancient shores of Sicilia and Sardinia, while not deserted, are closer to being ghost towns than the bustling centers of tourism, business and daily life they were just a few weeks ago.

Stores and shops have been shuttered. Restaurants and coffee shops no longer serve customers. Schools, universities, sporting arenas…even our museums and theaters…all closed. Even the Vatican City has closed its gates and armed patrols monitor the 20 foot tall walls that protect it!

Streets and roads are now empty for as far as the eye can see. Normally they would be filled with crazed Italian drivers in tiny cars and scooters (the ones that sound like demonic insects) darting here and there, reaching the limits of centrifugal force on our roundabouts. In the piazze of our towns and cities, there are now officially more pigeons than people. Many of us know someone who has been infected and recovered. Some of us know someone who did not recover…now they are dead. But everyone knows someone who has been affected by this microscopic monster in one way or another.

Sixty millions of us are in lockdown… it is like a war zone here. We are being held prisoner in our own homes by an unseen enemy that sneaked in unnoticed… by most of us. As you will read in just a few more minutes, there were those who knew something like this was coming… or at least they should have.

So who is to blame? With all this craziness swirling like a whirlpool at our feet, I just had to find the right answer. And so I have spent my free time (of which I have a lot these days) digging and researching.

I was literally shocked to discover how this has come to be. I am not going to bore you with talk of Patient '0' who spread it to

Patient '1' and how mathematics efficiently explains the rapid expansion of infection. No…I am going to tell you how (as I see it) the virus came to Italy.

It has everything to do with communism. Allow me to explain. Beginning in about 2014, Matteo Renzi, the imbecile ex-mayor of Firenze (Florence) acting as the leader of the Partito Democratico (synonymous with the Italian Communist party), somehow managed to get himself elected as Italy's Prime Minister. To give you a proper frame of reference, Matteo Renzi was so far left, he would make Barack Obama look like Barry Goldwater!

At the same time that Renzi was leading Italy into oblivion, strange things were happening in Italy's economy. Banks were failing…but not closing. Retirement ages were being extended…for some reason the pension funds were dwindling or disappearing. The national sales tax we call IVA (Value Added Tax) rose from 18% to 20%, then to 21% and again to 22%.

And in the midst of all this financial chicanery, the Chinese began furiously buying up Italian real estate and businesses in the North.

Now the reason I mention Renzi and the Chinese together is that strange things were also going on between the governments of Italy and China. A blind eye was being turned to the way the Chinese were buying businesses in the financial, telecommunication, industrial and fashion sectors of Italy's economy, all of which take place in Milano.

To be brief…China was getting away with purchases and acquisitions in violation of Italian law and EU Trade Agreements with the US and the UK…and no one in either of those countries (not Obama in the US or Cameron in the UK) said a thing in their country's defense. As a matter of fact, much of it was hidden from the public in all three countries. In 2014, China infused the Italian economy with €5 billion through purchases of companies costing less than €100 million each. By the time Renzi left office (in disgrace) in 2016, Chinese acquisitions had exceeded €52 billion. When the dust settled, China owned more than 300 companies...representing 27% of the major Italian corporations.

The Bank of China now owns five major banks in Italy...all of which had been secretly (and illegally) propped up by Renzi using pilfered pension funds! Soon after, the China Milano Equity Exchange was opened and much of Italy's wealth was being funneled back to the Chinese mainland.

Chinese state entities own Italy's major telecommunication corporation

(Telecom) as well as its major utilities (ENI and ENEL). Upon entry into the telecommunication market, Huawei established a facility in Segrate, a suburb of Milano. It launched it's first research center there and worked on the study of microwaves which has resulted in the possibly-dangerous technology we call 5G.

China also now owns controlling interest in Fiat-Chrysler, Prysmian and Terna. You will be surprised to know that when you put a set of Pirelli tires on your car, the profits are going to China. Yep...the Chinese colossus of ChemChina, a chemical industry titan, bought that company too!

Last but not least is Ferretti yachts...the most prestigious yacht builder in Europe. Incredibly, it is no longer owned by the Ferretti family.

But the sector in which Chinese companies invested most was Italy's profitable fashion industry. The Pinco Pallino, Miss Sixty, Sergio Tacchini, Roberta di Camerino and Mariella Burani brands have been acquired by 100%.

Designer Salvatore Ferragamo sold 16% and Caruso sold 35%. The most famous case is Krizia, purchased in 2014 by Shenzhen Marisfrolg Fashion Company, one of the leaders of high-priced, ready-to-wear fashions in Asia.

Throughout all of these purchases and acquisitions, Renzi's government afforded the Chinese unrestricted and unfettered access to Italy and its financial markets, many coming through without customs inspections.

Quite literally, tens of thousands of Chinese came in through Milano (illegally) and went back out carrying money, technology and corporate secrets.

Thousands more were allowed to enter and disappeared into shadows of Milano and other manufacturing cities of Lombardy, only to surface in illegal sewing shops, producing knock-off designer clothes and slapping 'Made In Italy' labels on them. All with the tacit approval of the Renzi government.

It was not until there was a change in the governing party in Italy that the sweatshops and the illegal entry and departure of Chinese nationals was stopped. Matteo Salvini, representing the Lega Nord party, closed Italy's ports to immigrants and systematically began disassembling the sweatshops and deporting those in Italy illegally.

But his rise to power was short-lived. Italy is a communist country...socialism is in the national DNA. Ways were found to remove Salvini, after which the communist party, under the direction of Giuseppe Conte, reopened the ports. Immediately, thousands of unvetted, undocumented refugees from the Middle East and East Africa began pouring in again. Access was again provided to the Chinese, under the old terms, and as a consequence thousands of Chinese, the majority from Wuhan, began arriving in Milano.

In December of last year, the first inklings of a coronavirus were noticed in Lombardy...in the Chinese neighborhoods. There is no doubt amongst senior medical officials that the virus was brought here from China.

By the end of January 2020 cases were being reported left and right. By mid-February the virus was beginning to seriously overload the Lombardy hospitals and medical clinics. They are now in a state of collapse.

The Far-Left politicians sold out and betrayed the Italian people with open border policies and social justice programs. One of the reasons the health care system collapsed so quickly is because the Renzi government (and now continued under the Conte government) redirected funds meant to sustain the medical system, to pay for the tens of thousands of immigrants brought in to Italy against the will of the Italian people.

If you remember the horrible earthquake that decimated the villages around Amatricia, in the mountains east of Rome in 2015, you would also remember how the world responded by sending millions of dollars to help those affected.

But there is a law in Italy that prevents private donations to charitable Italian organizations. All money and donations received must be turned over to a government agency, who in turn is to appropriate the funds as needed. But that agency is corrupt just as are all the others. Most of the money never reached a single victim in the mountains. The Renzi government redirected the vast majority of those funds to pay for the growing immigrant and refugee costs.

As the economy worsened under the burden of illegal immigration, compounded by gross government spending and incompetence, unemployment rose quickly…especially among young people. The unemployment rate for men and women under age 35 is close to 40%. So more money was diverted from the health care system and used to pay what is known here as guaranteed income. Whether you work or not you are paid here, especially if you belong to the PD! The government simply raises taxes on those who do work. Let me give you a quick example of the height of insanity to which Italian taxation has risen. If you live in a building that has a balcony or balconies…and any of those balconies cast a shadow on the ground, you must pay a public shadow tax! I will say no more!

The point I am trying to make here is that not only did the Chinese bring the virus to Italy (and the rest of the world) it was far-Left politics and policies that facilitated it.

This should hopefully be a warning to Americans that while they work to rid themselves of the China Virus, they should just as vehemently endeavor to rid their government of any politician that circumvents the Constitution and ignores the laws of the land… plain and simple.

UNQUOTE

Giacomino Nicolazzo is one of Italy's most beloved writers. Born and raised in Central Pennsylvania, he lives in a small village in Lombardy where he writes his books.

The second story refers to an interview Valuentainment – who is responsible ?

Interview by Patrick Bet-David, CEO of PHP Agency, Inc., emerging author and Creator of Valuetainment on Youtube with Danielle Dimartino Booth, CEO & Chief Strategist, Quill Intelligence LLC. Danielle Dimartino Booth said the following:

- In late November 2019, word had already gotten off the mainland that there was a virus in Wuhan. On December 15, 2019 the U.S Trade bill was signed.

- Six weeks later the Trade truce was signed with an out clause – a very clever out clause that the Chinese made sure was in there. They said that if there was any kind of act of God PANDEMIC, then they did not have to make good on what they had committed to buy from the U.S. Within days they announced the first coronavirus.

- Did the Chinese know damn well that this thing was running around the World for six weeks before they shut down Wuhan? Yes, they did. Is this criminal? YES, it is. Does it deserve to go in front of the World tribunal? Yes, it does. Because we know that it was the unfettered travel that made this thing a global phenomenon. It was impossible to contain.

- Six weeks they knew, but they wanted this out clause; and they under reported what happened in Wuhan which a toddler could tell you based on what happened in Italy; based on what's has happened in Germany and in France; and now in the U.K with Boris Johnson in the ICU.

- There is no way in a city the size of New York, 11million people that there were few cases, it's impossible with similar density to New York. So the WHO should be held responsible for not holding China accountable to providing good valid data so that the rest of the World could prepare for fewer people to die.

- To me these are equivalent to acts of war on the part of China

According to BBC News of 17 April, 17, 2020 Chinese city of Wuhan, where the coronavirus originated last year, has raised its official Covid-19 death toll by 50%, adding 1,290 fatalities. China has been accused of downplaying the severity of its virus outbreak; of course, China has insisted there was no cover-up. Wuhan's 11 million residents spent months in strict lockdown conditions, which have only recently been eased. The latest official figures bring the death toll in the city in China's central Hubei province to 3,869, increasing the national total to more than 4,600. China has confirmed nearly 84,000 coronavirus infections, the seventh-highest globally, according to Johns Hopkins University data. Why are there concerns over China's figures? In December 2019, Chinese authorities launched an investigation into a mysterious viral pneumonia after cases began circulating in Wuhan. China reported the cases to the World Health Organization (WHO), the UN's global health agency, on 31 December 31, 2019. But WHO experts were only allowed to visit China and investigate the outbreak on February 10, 2020, by which time the country had more than 40,000 cases. Around that time, a doctor who tried to warn his colleagues about an outbreak of a Sars-like virus was silenced by the authorities. This Doctor Li Wenliang later died from Covid-19. Wuhan's death toll increase of almost exactly 50% has left some analysts wondering if this is all a bit too neat.

What to do? Maybe go hug more Chinese and show your love for them, like the mayor of Florence at the expense of his country?

Out of contest, apart from fears, death and economic chaos Covid-19 has created, few significant happenings are:

+ Hong Kong protests have stopped. (resurfacing again thanks to China planning to introduce a new security laws)

+ Yellow-vast protests in France have disappeared.

+ Venezuela street protests are gone. Maduro's regime has been locked in a political crisis for more than a year, with the US and more than 50 other countries recognizing opposition leader Juan Guaido as the country's interim leader.

Naming a pandemic is not as easy or as straightforward as it might appear. The original name for coronavirus was nCoV-2019, which stood for novel coronavirus, discovered in 2019. The World Health Organization named it as "COVID-19." "COVI" comes from coronavirus. The "D" stands for disease. The 19 represents 2019, the year the virus was first identified, in December.

Interestingly, COVID – 19 could also read as **China Originated Virus In December 2019.** Once a crook, always a crook.

HISTORY OF PANDEMIC

1. HIV/AIDS PANDEMIC (AT ITS PEAK, 2005-2012)

Death Toll: 36 million

Cause: HIV/AIDS

First identified in Democratic Republic of the Congo in 1976, HIV/AIDS has truly proven itself as a global pandemic, killing more than 36 million people since 1981. Currently between 31 and 35 million people are living with HIV, the vast majority of those are in Sub-Saharan Africa, where 5% of the population is infected, roughly 21 million people. As awareness has grown, new treatments have been developed that make HIV far more manageable.

2. FLU PANDEMIC (1968)

Death Toll: 1 million

Cause: Influenza

A category 2 Flu pandemic sometimes referred to as "the Hong Kong Flu," the 1968 flu pandemic was caused by the H3N2 strain of the Influenza A virus, a genetic offshoot of the H2N2 subtype. From the first reported case on July 13, 1968 in Hong

Kong, it took only 17 days before outbreaks of the virus were reported in Singapore and Vietnam, and within three months had spread to Philippines, India, Australia, Europe, and the United States. While the 1968 pandemic had a comparatively low mortality rate (.5%) it still resulted in the deaths of more than a million people, including 500,000 residents of Hong Kong, approximately 15% of its population at the time.

3. ASIAN FLU (1956-1958)

Death Toll: 2 million

Cause: Influenza

Asian Flu was a pandemic outbreak of Influenza A of the H2N2 subtype, that originated in China in 1956 and lasted until 1958. In its two-year spree, Asian Flu traveled from the Chinese province of Guizhou to Singapore, Hong Kong, and the United States. Estimates for the death toll of the Asian Flu vary depending on the source, but the World Health Organization places the final tally at approximately 2 million deaths, 69,800 of those in the US alone.

4. FLU PANDEMIC (1918)

Death Toll: 20 -50 million

Cause: Influenza

Between 1918 and 1920 a disturbingly deadly outbreak of influenza tore across the globe, infecting over a third of the world's population and ending the lives of 20 – 50 million people. Of the 500 million people infected in the 1918 pandemic, the mortality rate was estimated at 10% to 20%, with up to 25 million deaths in the first 25 weeks alone. What separated the 1918 flu pandemic from other influenza outbreaks was the victims; where influenza had always previously only killed juveniles and the elderly or already weakened patients, it had begun striking down hardy and completely healthy young adults, while leaving children and those with weaker immune systems still alive.

5. PLAGUE AND SPANISH FLU (INDIA) – 1896 THRU 1918.

A dead rat thrown from the nearby Mauritius Fiji Emigration Depot caused the spread, T.S Ross, health officer of Madras in 1906, noted in his report. Plague rules then included:

+ Suspicious and confirmed cases were kept in isolation at hospitals, camps and homes.

+ Plague passports were issued to people who came from infected areas to Madras city

+ Special passes were given to those selling food and fuel

The Spanish flu was believed to have originated from influenza infected World War 1 troops returning home according to a 1914 research paper. 72,000 people died of plague until 1911-12 in

Madras Presidency alone. About 10 million deaths were reported due to Spanish flu in India alone.

World's Spanish death toll is estimated to have been anywhere from 17 million to 50 million, making it one of the deadliest pandemics in human history.

6. SIXTH CHOLERA PANDEMIC (1910-1911)

Death Toll: 800,000+

Cause: Cholera

Like its five previous incarnations, the Sixth Cholera Pandemic originated in India where it killed over 800,000, before spreading to the Middle East, North Africa, Eastern Europe and Russia. The Sixth Cholera Pandemic was also the source of the last American outbreak of Cholera (1910–1911). American health authorities, having learned from the past, quickly sought to isolate the infected, and in the end only 11 deaths occurred in the U.S. By 1923 Cholera cases had been cut down dramatically, although it was still a constant in India.

The Great Manchurian Plague that broke out across northeastern China in 1910 was devastating.

From the autumn of 1910, until the outbreak was finally suppressed the following year, an estimated 63,000 people died. This deadly epidemic spread through China and threatened to become a pandemic. Its origins appeared to be related to the trade in wild animals, but at the time no one was sure.

7. FLU PANDEMIC (1889-1890)

Death Toll: 1 million

Cause: Influenza

Originally the "Asiatic Flu" or "Russian Flu" as it was called, this strain was thought to be an outbreak of the Influenza A virus subtype H2N2, though recent discoveries have instead found the cause to be the Influenza A virus subtype H3N8. The first cases were observed in May 1889 in three separate and distant locations, Bukhara in Central Asia (Turkestan), Athabasca in northwestern Canada, and Greenland. Rapid population growth of the 19th century, specifically in urban areas, only helped the flu spread, and before long the outbreak had spread across the globe. Though it was the first true epidemic in the era of bacteriology and much was learned from it. In the end, the 1889-1890 Flu Pandemic claimed the lives of over a million individuals.

8. THIRD CHOLERA PANDEMIC (1852–1860)

Death Toll: 1 million

Cause: Cholera

Generally considered the most deadly of the seven cholera pandemics, the third major outbreak of Cholera in the 19th century lasted from 1852 to 1860. Like the first and second pandemics, the Third Cholera Pandemic originated in India, spreading from the Ganges River Delta before tearing through Asia, Europe, North America and Africa and ending the lives of over a million people. British physician John Snow, while working in a poor area of London, tracked cases of cholera and eventually succeeded in identifying contaminated water as the means of transmission for the disease.

9. THE BLACK DEATH (1346-1353)

Death Toll: 75 – 200 million

Cause: Bubonic Plague

From 1346 to 1353 an outbreak of the Plague ravaged Europe, Africa, and Asia, with an estimated death toll between 75 and 200 million people. Thought to have originated in Asia, the Plague most likely jumped continents via the fleas living on the rats that so frequently lived aboard merchant ships. Ports being major urban centers at the time, were the perfect breeding ground for the rats and fleas, and thus the insidious bacterium flourished, devastating three continents in its wake.

10. PLAGUE OF JUSTINIAN (541-542)

Death Toll: 25 million

Cause: Bubonic Plague

Thought to have killed perhaps half the population of Europe, the Plague of Justinian was an outbreak of the bubonic plague that afflicted the Byzantine Empire and Mediterranean port cities, killing up to

25 million people in its year long reign of terror. Generally regarded as the first recorded incident of the Bubonic Plague, the Plague of Justinian left its mark on the world, killing up to a quarter of the population of the Eastern Mediterranean and devastating the city of Constantinople, where at its height it was killing an estimated 5,000 people per day and eventually resulting in the deaths of 40% of the city's population.

11. ANTONINE PLAGUE (165 AD)

Death Toll: 5 million

Cause: Unknown

Also known as the Plague of Galen, the Antonine Plague was an ancient pandemic that affected Asia Minor, Egypt, Greece, and Italy and is thought to have been either Smallpox or Measles, though the true cause is still unknown. This unknown disease was brought back to Rome by soldiers returning from Mesopotamia around 165AD; unknowingly, they had spread a disease that would end up killing over 5 million people, decimating the Roman army.

** Medical science has made such tremendous progress that there is hardly a healthy human left – Aldous Huxley **

BIOLOGICAL WARFARE

This chapter contains extracts from an article published by Thomas J. Johnson, Associate Professor of Respiratory Care and Health Sciences and Division Director, Respiratory Care, School of Health Professions

Biological or Bio-warfare (BW) or Gem-warfare is the use of biological pathogens (bacteria, viruses, fungi, and toxins derived from living organisms to kill or incapacitate one's enemies. This includes Chemicals other than explosives such as asphyxiating or nerve gases, poisons, defoliants, etc.

From poisoned arrows (Scythians, and later the Viet Cong guerrillas) to poisoned wells (Sparta, Persia, Rome and others) to bombs with deadly bacteria (Japan, United States, Soviet Union and Iraq), the intentional use of biowarfare has been around for centuries.

Herodotus, a Greek historian of the fifth century B.C.E. describes the Scythians archers of the Black Sea as employing poison-tipped arrows. According to Herodotus, Scythians used the decomposed bodies of several venomous adders indigenous to their region, mixed human blood and dung into sealed vessels and buried this mixture until it was sufficiently putrefied.

This poison would certainly contain the bacteria of gangrene and tetanus (Clostridium perfringens and Clostridium tetani) while the venom would attack red blood cells, nervous system and could even induce respiratory paralysis. A Scythian archer had a range of over 1,600 feet and could launch about twenty arrows per minute

During the siege of the city-state of Athens by the Spartans in the Peloponnesian War a devastating epidemic broke out which killed thousands of Athenians. The famous historian Thucydides, writing between 431 B.C. and 404 B.C. reported, "it was supposed that Sparta poisoned the wells."

Most people remember Hannibal as the great leader of the Cathaginian Army. In 190 B.C.he won a great naval battle over Eumenes II of Pergomon using bio-warfare. Hannibal had earthen jars filled with venomous snakes, covered and taken on board his ships. When the enemy ships came within range, the earthen jars with the snakes were hurled at the enemy vessels where they broke discharging their terrifying occupants among the enemy sailors. The resulting chaos was effective and Hannibal won easily.

In the 14th Century, the Tartar army besieging the city of Kaffa (present day Feodosia in the Ukraine) used a combination of psychological warfare and bio-warfare. The ubiquitous rat and an outbreak of the bubonic plague among their own troops worked for the

Tartar army besieging Kaffa in 1346. Tartars catapulted bodies of plague victims over the walls of Kaffa in an attempt to initiate an epidemic upon the residents. The bubonic plague is primarily a disease of rats and other rodents. Only when they become very numerous in close contact with humans does the plague arise in man. The bites of the fleas (in this case the Oriental rat flea, Xenopsylla cheopis) transmit the disease to humans. Most probably, the fleas on the rats scavenging in the Tartar camp probably traveled on their hosts into the city Kaffa before the first Tartar died of the plague.

The defenders subsequently contracted the bubonic plague and abandoned the city to the Tartars. Merchants from Genoa had been trading in the Crimean port when the Tartars attacked. The surviving Genoese returned to Italy via their ships and most likely brought the plague to Europe. In October of 1347, the merchant ships docked in Genoa. The Genoese ships must have had stowaways -- rats. The rats with their fleas disembarked and proceeded to change the face of Europe forever.

Chroniclers of the period report that the plague had spread from Italy to Spain and northward to France.

By 1350, the plague was in Scandinavia. In more densely populated areas or cities such as Paris, Oxford and London almost 66% of the population was killed. Other, more isolated regions such as Bohemia were virtually unscathed since traders rarely ventured into them. The result of the introduction of the bubonic plague into Europe was devastating. There were too few people to work the land, estates lost financial power that, in turn, provided an opportunity for kings to centralize power. Teachers and tutors in universities died and, with them, learning. Hence the term Dark Ages.

Without an idea of what caused the disease or how it spread, people were helpless. The University of Paris Faculty of Medicine reported in March of 1345 that the alignment of planets caused the plague. Others proposed that the night air, swamps, or the burning of bodies during war poisoned the air. As a result, the plague would wreak havoc on Europe for the next four hundred years.

After an incubation period of 2 to 10 days, there is an abrupt onset of symptoms. These range from high fevers, headaches, muscle pain to nausea and vomiting. The bubo develops in the groin as the legs are the most commonly flea bitten part of the body. Dark skin eruptions often encircle the neck. The plague victim develops shock or low blood pressure with an ashen pallor. As the disease progresses limbs become black from gangrene. The plague is not transmissible from person-to-person unless the microorganism invades the victim's lungs in late stages of the disease where it becomes the pulmonic form of the disease. Untreated, the plague has a mortality rate of approximately 60%.

The pulmonic plague has a mortality rate of nearly 100%.

The first recorded "weaponized" biological agent in North America occurred during the French and Indian Wars (1754 to 1767). The agent was smallpox. The method of delivery was blankets not bombs. Sir Jeffrey Amherst who was the commander of British forces in North America formulated a plan to "reduce," as he so clinically expressed it, the size of the Native American tribes that were hostile to the crown.

In late Spring 1763 there was an outbreak of smallpox in the garrison of Fort Pitt. This produced a bacterial delivery system that the medical world would now refer to as a "fomite," an inanimate object capable of naturally containing or transporting an infectious agent. Blankets and a handkerchief laden with the pus or dried scabs from the smallpox sores of the infected British troops were collected in Fort Pitt's infirmary. These blankets and handkerchiefs were usually burned. This time they were collected and saved.

On June 24, 1763, one of Amherst's subordinates Captain Ecuyer ceremoniously gave the blankets and one handkerchief to the Indians invited to confer at the Fort. History does repeat itself. This is uncannily similar to the Trojan Horse, the "infection" which brought down Troy. Captain Ecuyer recorded rather chillingly in his diary, "I hope it will have the desired effect. "This "gift" may have had its intended effect.

Native American tribes in the Ohio Valley suffered a smallpox epidemic. It must be noted that the immunologically naive people are most vulnerable to diseases not indigenous to their region. Native American tribes across America experienced serious losses due to their contact with Europeans and their African slaves. Additionally, the use of fomites to transmit smallpox is inefficient compared to respirable aerosolized particles. Imagine how effective Amherst and Ecuyer would have been if they could have sprayed the Native American villages.

When we consider the dearth of knowledge regarding diseases and disease transmission, the biowarfare (BW) of Amherst and Ecuyer is ahead of its time. In one of those remarkable ironies of history, it was an English physician, Edward Jenner who discovered the smallpox vaccine in 1796. What is also remarkable is the fact that science did not discover the germ theory and how diseases are transmitted until the late 1870's. With the work of Louis Pasteur (1822-1895) and Robert Koch (1843-1910) and the subsequent development of microbiology in the late 19th century, it was finally possible to isolate, produce and weaponize biological agents.

Germany may be credited with opening of the modern biological warfare program during World War I. Covert operations in Romania infected sheep destined for export to Russia with anthrax. The

German Legation in Romania had laboratory vessels containing cultures confiscated. Subsequently, the Bucharest institute of Bacteriology and Pathology identified Bacillus anthracis (anthrax) and Bacillus mallei (Glanders, a respiratory tract infection of horses and mules). Meanwhile, German saboteurs in France infected horses and mules. Even before the American entry in to the war, covert German bacteria warfare was attempted in the United States with the contamination of animal feed and infection of horses intended for export.

In the period between the World Wars, there was an attempt to regulate warfare. This well-intentioned but ineffectual effort resulted in the Geneva Protocol. Thus the first attempt to limit the use of biologicals in warfare was the 1925 Geneva Protocol for the Prohibition of the Use in War of Asphyxiating, Poisonous or Other Gases and Bacteriological Methods of Warfare.18 While prohibiting the use of bio-weapons, the treaty did not seek to prevent the research, production, or possession. There was no provision for inspection. Many countries that ratified the protocol stipulated the right for retaliation. An interesting footnote to history, the United States did not ratify the Geneva Protocol until 1975.

Little known and yet remarkable in its scope is Japan's biological warfare program during World War II. Probably, the most extensive and most horrific biological weapons research and deployment occurred in Manchuria from 1932 until the end of the war. This program, innocuously entitled as Unit 731 was located in Pingfan Manchuria. Under the direction of Dr. Shiro Ishii from 1932 to 1942 and then Kitano Misaji from 1942 until 1945, Unit 731 employed a staff of over 3,000 scientists and technicians. Unit 731, sprawled over 150 buildings and five satellite camps. Additional sub-units were located in Mukden, Changchun and Nanking.

Experimentation on prisoners using Shigella (bacterial dysentery), Vibrio cholerae (cholera) and Yersinia pestis (the bubonic plague) was part of the Unit 731 program. At least 10, 000 prisoners died. Most from "experimental infection" and the remaining were executed after experiments for autopsy. Under interrogation, scientists and technicians admitted to 12 "field trials" of weaponized biologicals. Eleven Chinese cities were attacked with biological agents. These attacks ranged from water supply contamination to food contamination with cholera, anthrax, Salmonella and the plague. Cultures of these agents were sprayed from aircraft.

Unit 731 weaponized the plague in an interesting way. Plague infected rats were fed upon by laboratory bred fleas. The Japanese then collected the now infected fleas, containerized them and released them over Chinese cities from low flying aircraft. It was reported that up to 15 million fleas were released in each attack. Chinese National Health Administration attributed wartime plague epidemics on these attacks by the Japanese of Unit 731 conditions in China during the war precluded rigorous epidemiological and bacteriological data collection.

Bio-warfare is a two-edged sword. Unit 731 was so secret and the Japanese troops in China were so under-trained and unequipped to deal with biological weapons that Japanese casualties resulted from these attacks. In 1941, the attack on Changteh ostensibly resulted in nearly 10,000 cholera cases and 1,700 deaths among the Japanese troops. This may be the second disadvantage of BW: the difficulty in protecting one's own troops. Kitano Misaji terminated these "field trials" in 1942. Both the United States and the Soviet Union's Biological Warfare program owe their germination to the work of Unit 731. The Soviets captured Unit 731. US forces captured Shiro Ishii and Kitano Misaji and granted them immunity from war crimes if they divulged their BW secrets. The US had no research in either offensive or defensive BW early in World War II. Only when the intelligence agents of the Office for Strategic Services (OSS) discovered the activities of Unit 731 did the US initiate its own offensive germ warfare program at Camp Detrick, Maryland in late 1942.

The British secretly developed their own biological warfare program focused on anthrax. To test the effectiveness of weaponized anthrax delivered by a conventional bomb the British chose Gruinard Island off the coast of Scotland. The island was bombed in experiments to determine the best dispersal. Then in 1943, there was an outbreak of anthrax in sheep and cattle on the coast of Scotland that faced Gruinard Island. Attempts at decontamination by starting brushfires failed as spores of anthrax had been embedded in the island's soil thus making total decontamination impossible to this day. This creates the third disadvantage of BW use by a nation; the difficulty in decontamination may preclude the use of an acquired territory.

It is interesting to note that the Nazi offensive BW program limited itself to inhuman experiments not unlike Japan's Unit 731. Prisoners in Nazi concentration camps were forcibly infected with a wide variety of bacteria, protozoa and even a virus, Hepatitis A. These horrors were ostensibly experiments done to study pathogenesis and to develop vaccines and sulfa drugs rather than to develop weaponized versions of these pathogens. There is a positive note to this inhumanity; it was used against the Germans in an area of occupied Poland. Polish physicians in the region used a vaccine (formalin-killed Proteus OX-19) to produce a false-positive test for typhus. German troops were not dispatched to the area to round up its residents for deportation to concentration camps, thus saving an unknown number of people.

Meanwhile the US offensive biological warfare program was begun in 1942, under the Direction of the War Reserve Service, a civilian agency. It had research and development facilities at Camp Detrick, MD with production in Terre Haute, IN and testing in Mississippi and Utah. The Terre Haute production facility had inadequate engineering safety measures. This precluded large-scale biological weapons production. However the Camp Detrick "pilot plant" produced 5000 bombs of anthrax.

During the Korean War (1950 - 1953) new production facility at Pine Bluff, AR was constructed incorporating adequate biosafety measures. These safety systems are to protect the staff and the people and livestock in the vicinity. Additionally, a program to protect troops in the field with vaccines, anti-sera and therapeutic agents was initiated in 1953. Weaponization of microorganisms was begun in 1954.

The Cold War between the US and the USSR intensified with propaganda and an arms race unlike any the world has seen. At the United Nations General Assembly, the Soviet Union accused the United States of using germ warfare in Korea. It was this accusation that changed the focus of the US program. It also resulted in secret and controversial experiments.

The American program elected to use so-called "Surrogate Biological Agents" that were ostensibly non- pathologic to humans. These surrogates were used to simulate the employment of more deadly organisms. In a highly classified program bacterium such as Serratia marcescens and Bacillus subtilis (the classic college microbiology lab bacteria) were sprayed in US cities. The program was shut down in 1969. In the San Francisco experiment with Serratia marcescens 5,000 particles per minute were sprayed from the coast inward. One man died and ten others were hospitalized by an infection that was never followed up. Declassified information indicates that during the test there was five to ten times the normal infection rate in San Francisco areas that were sprayed.

More alarming were the tests to determine the vulnerability of the New York City subway system to biowarfare. In 1966, Bacillus subtilis was released into the subways. The results of this experiment showed that the release of an organism in just one station would infect the entire underground subway system due to winds and vacuum created by the passing subway trains.27 The declassified information was published in Leonard Cole's 1988 book, Clouds of Secrecy. One wonders if it was read by the cult Aum Shinrikyo for its planning of a nerve gas (sarin) attack on the Tokyo subway in March of 1995. The cult was weaponizing anthrax, botulinum and had even attempted to obtain the Ebola virus for a weapon.

Meanwhile in Southeast Asia, the spread of war created one clear use of biological warfare and several accusations. In Vietnam, the Communist Viet Cong guerrillas dug pits and implanted spikes of bamboo and other woods that were contaminated with human feces. These were called punji pits.29 The unwitting combatant or non-combatant who stepped into the pit was impaled upon the spikes and were inoculated with material that would produce a rapid and virulent infection.20 The Soviet Union was accused of using mycotoxins as "yellow rain" in support of communists armies in Cambodia and Laos. However there was no confirming evidence.

President Nixon signed National Security Decisions 35 and 44 in November of 1969 and February of 1970 terminating the United States offensive BW weapons program. This mandated the cessation of offensive BW research and the destruction of the BW arsenal. The only permitted research was defensive, such as diagnostic tests, vaccines and chemotherapies. As a direct result of the termination of the offensive BW program, the US Army Medical Research Institute for Infectious Disease (USAMRIID) was established at Ft. Detrick, MD. None of USAMRIID's research is classified. Nearly simultaneously in 1969 Great Britain submitted a proposal to the United Nations Committee on Disarmament. It includes a prohibition on the development, production and stockpiling of biological weapons. By 1972, the United Nations Convention on the Prohibition of the Development, Production, and Stockpiling of Bacteriological and Toxin Weapons and Their Destruction (BWC) was ratified by member nations. There were some notable violations.

The Soviet Union continued its offensive biological warfare program after signing the 1972 BWC under the title of Biopreparat. Under the Ministry of Defense, Biopreparat ran a minimum of 6 research laboratories with 5 weapons production facilities. At least 55,000 scientists and technicians worked for Biopreparat. Even with these resources there was a terrible failure of Biopreparat's biosafety systems.

Western intelligence agencies long suspected that the military facilities in the Soviet city of Sverdlovsk, now Ekaterinburg, Russia was a biological warfare research facility. In April 2, 1979, an outbreak of a disease that affected 94 people and killed at least 64 occurred in the city of Sverdlovsk located nearly 850 miles east of Moscow. The first victims died after 4 days and the last died 6 weeks later. People and animals in a narrow zone downwind of the facility were infected. Livestock as far away as 50 km from the facility died. The Soviet government reported that the deaths were caused by tainted meat, intestinal anthrax.32 Then 13 years later, President Boris Yeltsin admitted that the anthrax outbreak was the result of an unintentional release of anthrax.

The dispersal of the anthrax spores with the prevailing wind and the meteorological conditions was a classic plume. Considering that this was an accidental release and the effects were felt for 50 km, one must consider the range and causalities that would have resulted if this were a deliberate attack. Russia permitted a Western team of scientists that included Prof. Matt Meselson to visit Sverdlovsk in June 1992 and again in August 1993.34 Despite KGB confiscation of medical documents, the scientists were able to document that the victims were clustered in a straight line downwind of the facility. Of course they were not able to determine what exactly caused the release or what specific activities were being conducted at the Sverdlovsk military facility. This incident demonstrates the effectiveness of the first route of infection, inhalation.

The Cold War is responsible for the first documented modern assassination using a biological agent. In an operation out of the pages of an Ian Fleming's James Bond spy novel, the KGB and the Bulgarian secret police executed a flawless and as yet unsolved murder. Yuri Andropov, the chairman of the Soviet KGB reportedly authorized technical assistance and training for the operation. On September 7, 1978 Georgi Markov a Bulgarian writer and journalist who worked for the BBC and for Radio Free Europe left home for work at the BBC. It was his habit to take the Waterloo Bridge bus to the BBC headquarters. As Markov neared the queue of people waiting for the bus, he suddenly felt a stinging pain in the back of his right thigh. He turned and saw a heavyset man in his

40's stooping over to pick up a dropped umbrella. The man hailed a taxi and disappeared.

Unconcerned, Markov continued to work where he told his colleagues what happened. He showed one BBC friend a red pimple-like swelling on his thigh. That evening Markov developed a high fever and he was taken to a London hospital and treated for a non-specific type of blood poisoning. Three days later he was dead. On autopsy a tiny pellet was found in the wound in Markov's thigh. This pellet had an empty X-shaped cavity with two 0.34 mm holes. Toxicology results determined that Markov had been murdered by a poison, ricin. The ricin was encapsulated in a waxy base designed to melt at body temperature thus releasing into the tissues the ricin toxin. Ricin is a toxin that is derived from a plant source, a biological agent.

Ricin, the untreatable toxin of the Markov umbrella murder can be weaponized as an aerosol. With an average lethal dose of 1/5,000[th] of a gram it remains a potent BW agent. Under the 1972 Convention, it is defined as a "schedule one" controlled substance. Unfortunately, the worldwide processing of over 100,000,000 metric tons of castor beans results in a 5% waste mash. This waste mash is ricin toxin.37

While there were numerous claims that the Soviet Union employed mycotoxins, a.k.a. "yellow rain" in Cambodia, Laos and Afghanistan, there was no conclusive proof. Meteorological conditions, background fungal infections, and even bee pollen were confounding the findings of investigators. Then in September 1984 in Wasco county east of Portland, Oregon a cult called the Rashneeshee successfully contaminated the salad bars of 10 restaurants in the county. This second route of infection by a BW agent, the oral intake of contaminated food or water, resulted in 751 cases of salmonella poisoning. This was the first known bio-terrorist attack.

The Iran-Iraq War (1980-1988) was marked by numerous documented use of chemical weapons by Iraq. The UN Secretary General dispatched a team of specialists that conclusively verified allegations of Iraqi use of chemical agents to induce over 2,200 casualties. Despite numerous allegations of BW use by Iraq, the United Nations could not verify the reports.

As we have seen Biowarfare in its many forms is not new. From poisoning water to poisoning salad bars in restaurants, from poisoned arrows of 300 BC to poisoned punji stakes of the 1960s, from catapulting plague victims to dissemination of the plague by aircraft, warfare has included biological agents.

Thomas Johnson laments that the weaponization of these agents despite prohibitions will continue and the defense will run a parallel course. Will they be used again? It is only a question of when? Hopefully coronavirus is not from these BW experiments.

Most recent incident before the coronavirus happened in the U.K in 2018. On 4 March 2018, Sergei Skripal, a former Russian military officer and double agent for the UK's intelligence services, and his daughter Yulia Skripal were poisoned in Salisbury, Wiltshire, England, with a Novichok nerve agent, according to official UK sources and the Organisation for the Prohibition of Chemical Weapons (OPCW). After three weeks in a critical condition, Yulia regained consciousness and was able to speak. She was discharged on 9 April 2018. Sergei was also in a critical condition until he regained consciousness one month after the attack. He was discharged from hospital on 18 May 2018. A police officer was also taken into intensive care after apparent exposure to the remnants of the toxic agent at Sergei Skripal's residence. By 22 March he had recovered enough to leave the hospital.

Later on 12 March, the British government accused Russia of attempted murder and announced a series of punitive measures against Russia, including the expulsion of diplomats, on the 14 March. The UK's official assessment of the incident was supported by 28 other countries which responded similarly. Altogether, an unprecedented 153 Russian diplomats were expelled. Russia denied the accusations and responded similarly to the expulsions and "accused Britain of the poisoning.

On 5 September 2018, British authorities identified two Russian nationals, using the names Alexander

Petrov and Ruslan Boshirov, as suspected of the Skripals' poisoning and alleged that they were active officers in Russian military intelligence. On 8 October 2018, Investigative website Bellingcat revealed the real identity of the suspect named by police as Alexander Petrov to be Dr. Alexander Mishkin, also of the GRU. GRU is abbreviation of Glavnoye Razvedyvatelnoye Upravlenie, (Russian: Chief Intelligence Office), Soviet military intelligence organization

On 27 November 2019, the OPCW global chemical weapons watchdog added Novichok, the Soviet-era nerve agent used in the attack, to its list of banned toxins.

VIRUS & HINDU SCRIPTURES

According to Hindu Vedic cosmology there is no absolute start to time, as it is considered infinite and cyclic. Similarly, the space and universe have neither start nor end, rather it is cyclical. The current universe is just the start of a present cycle preceded by an infinite number of universes and to be followed by another infinite number of universes.

According to Vedic scriptures, there are three major causes for the diseases:

1. Annarasaja (diseases come from food),

2. Dosham (Refers to a bodily humor or bio-energy center) and

3. Krimijanya (diseases from pathogens and microbes).

Virus infections are Krimijanya. Krimi means worms, pathogens, and microbes. There are two types of krimis:

1. drishtah (that you can see with eyes or equipment) and

2. adristah (you can't see even with an ordinary microscope

Viruses come under the category of 'Achethanam' (life but no consciousness) whereas a human is under Chethanam (life with consciousness). As per Hindu scriptures, everything has life and the presence of divinity in it (Isavasyam idam sarvam).

Viruses are small obligate intracellular parasites, which by definition contain either a RNA or DNA genome surrounded by a protective, virus-coded protein coat. It develops 'chethana' the moment it gets into contact with a body with 'chethana'.

As modern humans, we inhabit the earth and destroy it for our pleasure. Similarly, a virus gets into our body considers it as just a host to inhabit and reproduce. Unlike humans, it doesn't consciously destroy the host. There are millions of viruses inside our body, happily living and co-existing. However, the body reacts to certain types of viruses only. When aggressive-reaction of the human body towards the external object creates the problem, we fall sick.

Our historic Epics (Ithihaas) Mahabharata says: "There are many creatures that are so minute that their existence can only be inferred. With the falling of the eyelids alone, they are destroyed."

The weight of a virus is measured at 0.85 attograms or 0.85 x 10-18 grams, or about one millionth of a trillion grams. 70 billion viruses that will make a person sick attract about 0.0000005 grams. Since the total number of cases worldwide is now over 2 million, the total weight of the rogue viruses that descend the world comes to about 1 gram. The entire mankind is on its knees with a total of 1 gram of virus!

Chhandogya Upanishad also discusses the birth of small creatures that live for a few hours and pass away. Their life is so short, of such an insignificant duration that one may say that they are born and then die. When you are seeing them being born, they are dead also at the same time. So short is the life of these creatures.

The entire universe has billions of viruses in it. You can't destroy them. They are much more powerful than human beings. They can mutate, become powerful and attack us again. So, the only way to survive is to prevent them from attacking us.

How to prevent viruses?

Simple - follow the Brahminical way of living. This has nothing to do with today's caste Brahmins. Brahminical way of living is irrespective of caste, sex, creed or religion. According to Upanishads, a Brahmana is who utters true speech, instructive and free from harshness and offends no one. A Brahmana (male/female) depends NOT on birth or lineage or family, but on just two factors - that is - Gyan (knowledge) and Tyag (sacrifice), says Gita.

Brahminical means just a scientific way of living with an understanding that everything is Brahmam (cosmos), which exists inside and outside. There is nothing other than Brahmam. It doesn't differentiate between humans and viruses. For Brahmam everything is inclusive. It doesn't destroy viruses to support human life. So please be aware that prayers won't work.

Hence, our ancestors have developed a way of life in tune with the Dharma of Brahmam. We call it the Dharmic way. (Dharma = duty, responsibility, right, and privilege together).

1. Get up at Brahma Muhurta (Some people call it Saraswati Yamam) - that's up to 48 minutes before Sunrise. After your daily routines, expose yourself to the rising sun and do Surya namaskar if possible, offering gratitude to sun or Gods that you believe. If you are non-believer, just be thankful for solar energy. According to Hindu scriptures, Surya is depicted as the destroyer of Krimis (pathogenic organisms).

2. After the bath, don't touch anyone and don't let others touch you. Respect all saying 'Namaste', with a slight bow and hands pressed together, palms touching and fingers pointing upwards, thumbs close to the chest.

3. Light lamp - after bath light lamp with sesame oil or ghee in front of your favorite God. Agni (fire) by its intense power destroys organisms and other agents that are harmful to the body says our scriptures.

4. Eat ONLY sattvik food. What's sattvik food? Broadly people say it is non-violent food,

avoiding parts of a dead body, hence vegetarian food.

5. As per Hindu custom, there was no dining table concept and people were eating sitting on the floor. Perform a ritual called ChitrAhuti before eating food - just sprinkle water around our plate (or plantain leaves) before starting our lunch.. It is just to prevent insects and mainly ants coming on to the food plate. Also, drink a mouthful of water before eating. Sitting on the floor and eating is regarded as a "sukhasan" position. This position while eating helps in improving digestion as the brain focuses solely upon digestion; not on our legs dangling from a chair or supporting us while we are standing.

6. From our childhood, we were not permitted to allow our lips to touch the cup or bottle from which we drank tea or water. The taboos include not sharing plates, not taking bites off each other's food. Now we know we have to follow these 'superstitions' strictly to avoid diseases.

7. If one goes to hair-cutting & beauty salon (Barber shop) for haircut or fixing nails, you are directed to go straight into a bath or shower.

8. Guests are always invited to first wash up as soon as they come in. It is customary to keep a bucket full of water or a pipe-outlet. We are supposed to wash our legs, hands, and face before entering into the house

9. Children playing outdoors are instructed to wash hands, feet, and face before settling down for homework or dinner..

10. Sleep on the floor over coir-mat or on wooden bedstead or on Charpoy a bed consisting of a frame strung with coir (Cot bedstead with coir woven bedding). This is sort of hard bedding with pressure points to eliminate back-pain, muscle tension or spondylitis and release blocked nerves naturally.

11. If there is a birth in the family, members of the family need to follow certain protocol of isolation for 10 days; this is to ensure that new born is safe from any contagious means.

12. Cremation of the dead. It is a method of final disposition of a dead body through burning in a pyre by combustion in a closed furnace (cremator), at a crematorium. Cremation is the practice of disposing of a corpse by burning. This is to avoid health risk to the living (No virus risk as everything is consumed in fire)

Ayurveda, the science of longevity is the earliest school of medicine known to humans. Charka, the father of medicine consolidated Ayurveda 2,500 years ago. Shastrakarma, is the art of surgery. Sushruta is the father of surgery. 2,600 years ago he and health scientists of his time conducted complicated surgeries like cesareans, cataract, artificial limps, fractures, urinary stones and even plastic surgery and brain surgery. Usage of anesthesia was well known in ancient India.

'Shanti mantra' mentions the importance of Brahmin in life. The sloka as a whole reads as follows:

"Swasti prajabhya: paripalayantham nyayeana margena mahim maheesah

gobrahmanebhya shubamsthu nityam lokah samastha sukhino bhavanthu

Om santhi, santhi santhihi"

It says only if cattle and the Brahmins have been well looked after, then all the beings in all the world become happy. It also says our Kings (the politicians and leaders) should be Dharmic.

So, it is simple, live like a Brahmin and avoid caste, religion, race, and creed; follow Vedic dharma which says "Vasudhaiva Kutumbakam" = the world as one family. Let's care and share.

Unfortunately, Brahminical way of living is a myth with Globalization. Virus infections (Krimijanya) are also man-made.

Kautilya's Arthashastra, an Indian manual on statecraft and military strategy, circa 400 BCE, encloses numerous recipes for making poison weapons and other chemical weapons. Interestingly, another manual of the same time period, the Laws of Manu, forbids the use of poison arrows.

As we progress further in this era (Kali Yuga), most of our fundamental belief systems are getting questioned and are shaken up from the root, targeting at destroying our rituals, observances, beliefs and our Sanatana Dharma itself. The arguments for and against such things - including those on the Social Media - has been driving many Hindus crazy. This behavior change might seem so logical, rational and obviously acceptable to the current and future generations - as we are brought up in the modern education system, which teaches us to question everything and accept only if it is proven scientifically or logically.

However, we need to take a pause and realize that we are coming far away from our roots - which happen to be super-science, proven time and again right by Science itself - only after being ridiculed initially for a few decades. While we may find it hard to accept it by the defines of rational thought, most of the current generation requires explanations and answers - at least something logical, for them to reason it out.

Here are few reasons to reinforce that ancient India (Bharat) are based on so called science:

+ People are advised to worship Neem and Banyan tree in the morning. Inhaling the air near these trees is good for health.

+ If you are trying to look ways for stress management, there can't be anything other than Hindu Yoga aasan Pranayama (inhaling and exhaling air slowly using one of the nostrils)

✦ Hindu temples are built scientifically. The place where an idol is placed in the temple is called 'Moolasthanam'. This 'Moolasthanam' is where earth's magnetic waves are found to be maximum, thus benefiting the worshipper.

✦ Every Hindu household has a Tulsi plant. Tulsi or Basil leaves when consumed, keeps our immune system strong to help prevent the H1N1 disease.

✦ The rhythm of Vedic mantras, an ancient Hindu practice, when pronounced and heard are believed to cure so many disorders of the body like blood pressure.

✦ Hindus keep the holy ash in their forehead after taking a bath, this removes excess water (moisture) from your head.

✦ Women keep kumkum bindi on their forehead that protects from being hypnotised.

✦ Eating with hands might be looked down upon in the west but it connects the body, mind and soul, when it comes to food.

✦ Hindu customs requires one to eat on a leaf plate (banana, palash leaves). This is the most eco-friendly way as it does not require any chemical soap to clean it and it can be discarded without harming the environment.

✦ Piercing of baby's ears is actually part of acupuncture treatment. The point where the ear is pierced helps in curing Asthma.

- ✦ Sprinkling turmeric mixed water around the house before prayers and after. Its known that turmeric has antioxidant, antibacterial and anti-inflammatory qualities.

- ✦ The old practice of pasting cow dung on walls and outside their house prevents various diseases/viruses as this cow dung is anti-biotic and rich in minerals.

- ✦ The age-old punishment of doing sit-ups while holding the ears actually makes the mind sharper and is helpful for those with Autism, Asperger's Syndrome, learning difficulties and behavioral problems.

- ✦ Decorating the main door with 'Toran'- a string of mangoes leaves. neem leaves, ashoka leaves actually purifies the atmosphere.

- ✦ Touching your elder's feet keeps your backbone in good shape.

- ✦ Cremation or burning the dead is one of the cleanest forms of disposing off the dead body.

- ✦ Chanting the mantra 'Om' leads to significant reduction in heart rate which leads to a deep form of relaxation with increased alertness.

INDIA & COVID - 19

India's coronavirus status on a population of 1.3 billion is about 186,000 cases and 5,300 fatal by May 31, 2020. There is a lot of speculation and eyebrows raised as to why this is so. Various reasons are being put out:

1. Arguments on non-availability or lack of testing facilities.

2. The Indian curry might have ingredients that are antiviral.

3. Maybe the high level of chillies (spices) in our food helps prevent lung infection by C-19.

4. The Indian habit of washing their hands and everything else may play a role.

5. The "Namaste" helps, as people don't touch each other, like hand-shake or hug each other. (Namaste is slight bow and hands pressed together, palms touching and fingers pointing upwards, thumbs close to the chest)

6. Indians are a lot vegetarian

India's lockdown is initiated in four phases so far

Phase 1: March 25, 2020 – April 14, 2020 (21 days)

Phase 2: April 15, 2020 – May 03, 2020 (19 days)

Phase 3: May 04, 2020 – May 17, 2020 (14 days)

Phase 4: May 18, 2020 - May 31, 2020

In phase 4 Government listed considerable relaxations in non-containment zones that are set to further open up the economy. Domestic air travel resumed from May 25, 2020 but with considerable restrictions.

Phase 5: June 01, 2020 – June 30, 2020

In this phase Government of India has released a list of new guidelines dubbing it *"Unlock 1"*, which will have an economic focus with plan to unlock in phases

Non-containment Zones:

- Places of worship (large religious gatherings are still not allowed), shopping malls, and hotels and restaurants can open from June 8

- Removes restrictions on inter- and intra-state travel.

- All activities that were prohibited earlier will be opened up in areas in a phased manner, with the stipulation of following Standard Operating Procedures (SOPs), to be prescribed by the Health Ministry.

- In the second phase of *Unlock 1*, the government plans to reopen all educational institutes including schools and colleges, after holding discussions with states and Union Territories. A decision is likely in July.

- International air travel, metro rail services, cinema halls, gyms, swimming pools, bars, entertainment parks, and auditoriums will remain closed and open only in the third phase of *Unlock 1*.

- Large gatherings, including social, political, religious, and sporting events are also banned for now.

- The third phase of the un-lockdown plan will focus on the resumption of these activities. No date, however, has been set for this.

- Night curfew prohibiting non-essential travel will be between 9 pm and 5 am

- Like the previous guidelines, the fresh one too advises people above 65, children below 10, pregnant women and those with underlying health conditions to stay indoors.

- The government has reiterated its advice for downloading the contact-tracing Aarogya Setu app, saying it "enables early identification of potential risk of infection".

- Face covers are mandatory in public places, asked people to maintain a distance of at least six feet, and reiterated that spitting and the consumption of paan, gutkha, tobacco and liquor in public places are not allowed. Weddings can be held with a maximum 50 guests and funerals with 20 people in attendance.

- Though there are no restrictions on offices, they have been asked to promote the idea of working from home as far as possible and put emphasis on staggered work hours.

- "With a view on ensuring safety in offices and work places, employers on best effort basis should ensure that Aarogya Setu is installed by all employees having compatible mobile phones," the guidelines said.

Containment zones:

Termed the epicentre of an infection, will continue to be under a hard lockdown at least till June 30, 2020. The Centre has empowered states/ Union Territories to identify containment zones in accordance with health ministry guidelines. Local authorities can also identify buffer zones, which are areas adjoining containment zones, and impose restrictions

WHO has commented that India will hit "peak" by July 2020. Major concern is pockets of slums in every State and movement of migrant laborers.

Thaipusam or Thaipoosam, is a festival celebrated by the Tamil community on the full moon in the

Tamil month of Thai (January/February). It is mainly observed in countries where there is a significant presence of Tamil community such as India, Sri Lanka, Malaysia, Mauritius, Singapore, South Africa, Canada and other places where ethnic Tamils reside as a part of the local Indian diaspora population such as Réunion, Indonesia, Thailand, Myanmar, Trinidad and Tobago, Guyana, Suriname, Jamaica and the other parts of the Caribbean. It marks the celebration of God Kartik's birthday with the usual gathering of few 100,000s. No epidemic, nothing happens year after year.

In India millions attend:

- Ratha Yatra, also known as Chariot festival in June or in July each year in the State of Odisha

- Kumbh Mela in north India

- Pushkaraalu in north India

- Sabari Mala in Kerala on pilgrimage

- River Ganges, millions take bath

Thousands pray together at Sri Harmandir Sahib, Gurudwaras in Punjab & Temples (like Tirupathi, Shirdi, and Rameswaram etc). Even eat together At Langar in Golden Temple, Punjab.

The Mumbai Suburban serve the Mumbai Metropolitan Region spread over 390 kilometres carries more than 7.5 million commuters daily. In Mumbai's Dharavi (Largest slum in Asia), 800,000 people live huddled in an area of 2.1 sq.Kms.

Not a single virus was born or spread. No Cholera outbreak or Typhoid or even E.Coli epidemic.

Possibly, the environment we Indians indulge in (means with aggarbattis (incense stick), Sandal wood paste (chandan), camphor, use of sesame oil for lighting lamps, extensive use of Mango leaves for Pooja (Prayers) and all associated smoke play a part in deterring its spread.

What do we, Indians do? TAKE PRECAUTIONS, DO NOT Panic & Don't forward rumours. All the prophets of doom and gloom surface in such occasions along with self-styled astrologers and fake news experts. The media and these self-declared experts generally like a calamity for their day under the sun.

On call of Indian P.M for Janta curfew on March 22, 2020, Lockdown began from March 25, 2020 at midnight and got extended initially till May 3, 2020 totaling to 40 days. There was overwhelming and spontaneous support from the Public. Also, please think over it:

Who is bringing stranded Indians from outside:

Indian Navy and India Air force and much maligned Air India; not other airlines.

Who is checking people at arrival:

Government servants; not private employees or IT packaged earners

Who is manning isolation centres:

Defence services and Government health workers and government hospitals; not private luxury hospitals.

Who is working day and night even when Gods have shut their places:

Government doctors and health workers; not private 6 digit salary earners..

Devising forces can never succeed with India; there are riverboat clinics which operate on the Brahmaputra serving remote villages in the NE. There is a guy called Dr Harish Hande (IIT KGP+ MIT+Magsaysay award) who is doing pioneering work in the field of solar power for rural areas of India. He is currently working with the river boat clinics to provide solar power for these boats. A lot of interesting good work is happening around us. Makeshift hospitals out of railway coaches is yet another example. When calamity approaches discrimination departs.

India started bringing their stranded citizens from May 07, 2020, mostly those who have lost their jobs, a massive repatriation process ever (named Vande Bharat) with 14 Indian Navy ships and 500 flights including 30 jumbos of the Indian Air Force. 11 million Indians are working in Middle East (M.E) countries and the majority are from the United Arab Emirates (UAE) and Saudi Arabia. Keralites waiting to be repatriated from M.E as of early May 2020 is around 200,000. Job losses in M.E as listed by Kerala Government is

415,000. This is just Keralites; there are good numbers from other states too. This evacuation process includes bringing stranded Indians from 31 Countries in all.

Janta curfew for 40 days (Phase 1 & 2 of lockdown) has some interesting connections. The Latin root of the word "quarantine" is "forty". In 1348, Venice was the first contemporary city to enforce an official quarantine in hopes of curbing transmission of bubonic plaque. Incoming travelers had to stay in isolation for "quaranta" (forty) days, hence where we derive the word 'quarantine".

- 40 stanzas of Hanuman Chalisa. Reciting the Hanuman Chalisa calls upon Hanuman's divine involvement in critical problems, including those concerning evil spirits.

- Mandal kal means a period of 40 days.

- The Sindhi Hindu community commemorates a festival of thanks to God called Chaliha Sahib. It lasts for 40 days.

- What does the BIBLE say about No. 40? The flood lasted 40 days. Moses stayed with God 40 days. Moses fled to Midian @ 40 years. Exodus lasted 40 years. Jonah declared God's wrath upon Nineveh after 40 days. JESUS fasted 40 days

Gautama Buddha fasted 40 days and nights in the wilderness and was tempted by evil spirits.

- Prophet Muhammad fasted 40 days in a cave.

- Muslims fast and pray for 40 days during the Ramzan period.

- Devotees of Swami Ayyappa visit Sabarimala temple after observing 40 days of fasting.

- Guru Nanak spent 40 days with a sufi saint in Nohria Bazar.

So a group of theologians think & say that the No. 40 represents "Change ".

Fascinating story of the connection between Hydroxychloroquine, British India, Srirangapatna and Gin & Tonic.

As most of us are already aware, Hydroxychloroquine has taken the world by storm. Every newspaper is talking about it, and all countries are requesting India to supply it. Now, a curious person might wonder why and how this chemical composition is so deeply entrenched in India, and is there any history behind it.

Well, there is an interesting history behind it which goes all the way to Tipu Sultan's defeat. In 1799, when Tipu was defeated by the British, the whole of Mysore Kingdom with Srirangapatnam as Tipu's capital, came under British control. For the next few days, the British soldiers had a great time celebrating their victory, but within weeks, many started feeling sick due to Malaria, because Srirangapatnam was a highly marshy area with severe mosquito trouble.

The local Indian population had over the centuries, developed self immunity, and also all the spicy food habits helped to an extent. Whereas the British soldiers and officers who were suddenly exposed to harsh Indian conditions, started bearing the brunt.

To quickly overcome the mosquito menace, the British Army immediately shifted their station from Srirangapatnam to Bangalore (by establishing the Bangalore Cantonment region), which was a welcome change, especially due to cool weather, which the Brits were gavely missing ever since they had left their shores. But the malaria problem still persisted because Bangalore was also no exception to mosquitoes.

Around the same time, European scientists had discovered a chemical composition called "Quinine" which could be used to treat malaria, and was slowly gaining prominence, but it was yet to be extensively tested at large scale. This malaria crisis among British Army came at an opportune time, and thus Quinine was imported in bulk by the Army and distributed to all their soldiers, who were instructed to take regular dosages (even to healthy soldiers) so that they could build immunity. This was followed up in all other British stations throughout India, because every region in India had malaria problem to some extent.

But there was a small problem. Although sick soldiers quickly recovered, many more soldiers who were exposed to harsh conditions of tropical India continued to become sick, because it was later found that they were not taking doses of Quinine. Why? Because it was very bitter!! So, by avoiding the bitter Quinine, British soldiers stationed in India were lagging behind on their immunity, thereby making themselves vulnerable to Malaria in the tropical regions of India.

That's when all the top British officers and scientists started experimenting ways to persuade their soldiers to strictly take these dosages, and during their experiments, they found that the bitter Quinine mixed with Juniper based liquor, actually turned somewhat into a sweet flavor. That's because the molecular structure of the final solution was such that it would almost completely curtail the bitterness of Quinine.

That juniper based liquor was Gin. And the Gin mixed with Quinine was called "Gin & Tonic", which immediately became an instant hit among British soldiers.

The same British soldiers who were ready to even risk their lives but couldn't stand the bitterness of Quinine, started swearing by it daily when they mixed it with Gin. In fact, the Army even started issuing few bottles of Gin along with "tonic water" (Quinine) as part of their monthly ration, so that soldiers could themselves prepare Gin & Tonic and consume them every day to build immunity.

To cater to the growing demand of gin & other forms of liquor among British soldiers, the British

East India company built several local breweries in and around Bengaluru, which could then be transported to all other parts of India. And that's how, due to innumerable breweries and liquor distillation factories, Bengaluru had already become the pub capital of India way back during British times itself. Eventually, most of these breweries were purchased from British organizations after Indian independence, by none other than Vittal Mallya (Vijay Mallya's father), who then led the consortium under the group named United Breweries headquartered in Bengaluru.

Coming back to the topic, that's how Gin & Tonic became a popular cocktail and is still a popular drink even today. The Quinine, which was called Tonic (without gin), was widely prescribed by Doctors as well, for patients who needed cure for fever or any infection. Whenever someone in a typical Indian village fell sick, the most common advice given by his neighbors was "Visit the doctor and get some tonic". Over time, the tonic word was so overused that became a reference to any medicine in general. So, that's how the word "Tonic", became a colloquial word for "Western medicine" in India.

Over the years, Quinine was developed further into many of its variants and derivatives and widely prescribed by Indian doctors. One such descendent of Quinine, called Hydroxychloroquine, eventually became the standardized cure for malaria because it has relatively lesser side effects compared to its predecessors, and is now suddenly the most sought after drug in the world today.

And that's how, a simple peek into the history of Hydroxychloroquine takes us all the way back to Tipu's defeat, mosquito menace, liquor rationing, colorful cocktails, tonics and medicinal cures.

The world is looking for "Hydroxychloroquine" for treatment of Covid19 and India is the leading manufacturer of Hydroxychloroquine.

The man behind Hydroxychloroquine is Acharya Prafulla Chandra Roy, known as "The father of Indian Chemistry", who was a well-known Indian Scientist, teacher and one of the first modern Indian chemical researchers. Government of India has issued a commemorative postal stamp on him.

He discovered the stable compound mercurous nitrate in 1896. In 1901 Bengal Chemicals was formed by him, which is the first pharmaceutical company in India, and this pharma company is the leading manufacturer of Hydroxychloroquine.

CIPLA Pharma creation reads similar to Acharya Prafulla Chandra Roy's story, In the 1920s, a rich man in India put his son on board a ship from Bombay to the United Kingdom in order to acquire a law degree and become a barrister, as was fashionable among all privileged families in the country at the time. The boy, however, did not want to be a lawyer; his heart was in chemistry, a pursuit without a seeming future in those days.

But his father gave him little choice, so while he waved to his father as his ship pulled away, Khwaja Abdul Hamied was already running over other plans in his mind while standing on the deck. He jumped ship halfway through the seas to land in Germany which, in the early decades of the last century, was leading in the study of chemistry and chemicals. He acquired a degree, married a German Jew. Before they could be caught by Adolf Hitler's Gestapo, they escaped from Germany and safely reached India.

With his vast knowledge of chemicals, Khwaja Hamied set up the Chemical, Industral and Pharmaceutical Laboratories in 1935 which was shortened to CIPLA decades later after Independence.

Khwaja Hamied got down, in true nationalist spirit, to producing cheaply priced generic drugs for the common people. These included not only medicines for malaria and tuberculosis but also other respiratory disorders, cardiovascular diseases as well as routine and mundane ailments like diabetes and arthritis.

Sometime in the 1970s, CIPLA (so renamed in the 1980s) began to manufacture a drug called Propranolol, patented by a US pharmaceutical giant from Brooklyn in New York, that was used in treating blood pressure, migraines and heart ailments, among others. In a bipolar world at the time, the US was no friend of India and a real superpower.

The US complained to the Indian government. The then Prime Minister Indira Gandhi did not immediately cave in. She sent for Yusuf Hamied, Khwaja's son, himself a chemistry graduate from Cambridge, who had by then taken over the running of the company. When Mrs Gandhi asked how he could violate the patent law on drugs and get India into trouble, Yusuf told Mrs Gandhi the story of his father and why he had set up the company – to bring low priced quality drugs to the poor.

When he had handed his company to his son, Khwaja had told Yusuf just one thing – remember why this company was founded. "Unlike other pharmaceutical companies around the world, we are not here to make profits but to bring relief and healthcare to the poor who may otherwise have to die for want of quality drugs."

Yusuf told an impressed Mrs Gandhi who could empathize with the concern for the poor. And she turned down the US's command to India to stop producing the drug, knowing it could have consequences. Americans hated her for this and other acts of defiance, but she always had the interests of her own fellow citizens on top priority.

On Yusuf's suggestion she also had the patent law on drugs changed to not include the drug per se, only the process of manufacture as inviolable, so that Cipla could go ahead and produce as many low-priced generic drugs for the poor as possible. Since then Cipla has also produced a low-cost drug to treat HIV and expanded operations into several developing countries, including African nations, where most HIV and poor patients existed at one time.

Today, the world is reeling from the COVID-19 crisis and the vulnerable segments of our society are the most at risk. Hydroxychloroquine has emerged as the most sought-after medicine after preliminary trials in China suggested it boosted recovery and lowered the severity of the coronavirus disease. India is the world's largest manufacturer of this drug. India is allowing limited exports of the anti-malaria hydroxychloroquine on humanitarian grounds. The limited exports were allowed after US president Donald Trump requested the supply of the drug from India in a phone call with Prime Minister Narendra Modi early in April 2020. This export has been extended to Brazil as well.

Whole world is advising on "social distancing" to mitigate the spread of coronavirus. Social distancing and Lock-down is a privilege:

- It means you live in a house large enough to practice it.

- Hand washing is a privilege too. It means you have access to running water.

- Hand sanitizers are a privilege. It means you have money to buy them.

- Lockdowns are a privilege. It means you can afford to be at home.

- Most of the ways to ward the Corona off are accessible only to the affluent.

In essence, a disease that was spread by the folks as they flew around the globe will now kill millions of the poor.

All of us who are practicing social distancing and have imposed a lockdown on ourselves must appreciate how privileged we are. Many Indians especially those Below Poverty Line (BPL) won't be able to do any of this.

Everything is not locked down

Sunrise is not locked down

Love is not locked down

Family time is not locked down

Kindness is not locked down

Creativity is not locked down

Learning is not locked down

Conversation is not locked down

Imagining is not locked down

Reading is not locked down

Relationship is not locked down

Praying is not locked down

Meditation is not locked down

Sleeping is not locked down

Work from home is not locked down

Faith and Hope is not locked down

Today, lock-down, social distancing and quarantine are the words extensively mentioned in the media. Millions of people around the world are under isolation orders to prevent the spread of coronavirus,

Meet a man who has lived alone on an island for 31 years. Mauro Morandi has lived alone on Italy's Budelli Island for 31 years. "What I love the most is the silence," he says. In 1989, Mauro Morandi's catamaran—engine crippled and anchor adrift—washed up on the Coast of Budelli Island, located on a stretch of water between Sardinia and Corsica. As luck would have it, Morandi learned that the island's caretaker was retiring from his post, so he sold his boat and assumed a new role. Thirty-one years later, Morandi remains the sole resident and guardian of the island.

Isolation is not new to India. Fourteen years of Vanavaas (living in a forest) in isolation in our Vedic epics Ramayana and Mahabharata is well known.

With vehicles off the city roads and most industries shut for over a month due to the coronavirus induced lockdown; there is dramatic drop in air pollution levels

- Air quality in Mumbai has improved significantly. A study, 'Impact of Lockdown (March 25 to April 19) on Air Quality', undertaken by the Central Pollution Control Board (CPCB) shows a sharp decrease of 77 per cent in nitrogen dioxide (NO2) levels and 59 per cent drop in average benzene (a hydrocarbon, C6H6) level during the lockdown period as compared to the weeks preceding it.

- From Jalandhar one can Snow-Capped Himachal Mountains 200 Kms away for first time in decades.

- Brahma Kamals have bloomed near Badrinath. A sight which had not been seen since decades!

Animal kingdom is trying to reclaim its lost property. There are several sightings.

- In the holy mountain range Thirumala, peacocks, deers and wild-pigs, tiger, cheetah etc have started roaming around roads leading to the Lord Venkateswara Temple as human traffic has completely stopped due to lockdown.

- In Chembur, Mumbai golf club, lilies have bloomed in ponds.

- Dolphins are sighted off Chennai and Mumbai coasts

- Peacocks from Mud Island have started coming to the suburbs off Kandivali in Mumbai.

Government of India has launched *"Aarogya Setu"*, the COVID-19 tracking mobile application developed by the National Informatics Centre. The purpose of this application is to spread awareness of COVID-19 and to connect essential COVID-19 - related health services to the people of India. It is a tracking application which uses the smartphone's GPS and Bluetooth features to track the coronavirus infection.

When calamity approaches discrimination departs.

To help those Below Poverty Line (BPL) Indian Government has come out with a scheme, Garib Kalyan Yojana 2020, briefly benefits include:

Beneficiary	Amount/benefit
Ration cardholder (800 Million people)	5 kg ration free of cost additionally
Corona warriors (doctors, nurse, staff)	INR 5 Million insurance
Jan Dhan account holders (women's)	INR 500/- from next three months
Widower, poor citizens, disabled, senior citizens	INR 1000/- (for next three month)
Employees Provident Fund (EPF)	24% (12% +12%) will be paid by the government for the next three months. Also, amendments will be made to the Employees' Provident Fund Organisation (EPFO) Scheme so that organised sector workers can withdraw the non-refundable advance. Up to three months' salary or 75% of the amount available, whichever is lower, can be withdrawn. This move will benefit around 48 Million workers who are part of the Employees Provident Fund (EPF) scheme.

Beneficiary	Amount/benefit
Direct Debit Transfer (DBT)	Cash transfer via DBT will be provided by the government to households, women, women under Jan Dhan Yojana, Divyang, poor pensioners, widows, Mahatma Gandhi National Rural Employment Guarantee Act (MNREGA) workers, and farmers. An increase in wages will be provided for MNREGA workers. According to the government, this move will help 50 Million families. An increase in wage will lead to an additional income of INR 2,000 for every worker.
Ujjawala Scheme	Cylinder free of cost for the next three months
Women Self-Help Groups (SHGs)	Will get an extra 10 lakh collateral loan
Construction worker	INR 310,000 Million fund will be used for them

Further to the above, in his address to the Nation on May 12, 2020, announced further measures:

+ Self-Reliant India Movement ("Atmanirbhar Bharat"), Five pillars of – Economy, Infrastructure, System, Vibrant Demography and Demand

+ Special economic and comprehensive package of INR 20 Lakh Crores (INR 20 Billion) -equivalent to 10% of India's GDP

+ Package to cater to various sections including cottage industry, Micro, Small, & Medium Enterprises (MSMEs), labourers, middle class, industries, among others.

+ Bold reforms across sectors will drive the country's push towards self-reliance

+ It is time to become vocal for our local products and make them global.

INDIA'S LESSONS TO THE WORLD

Covid – 19 has given rise to Hybrid Warfare, a strategy that employs political warfare and blends conventional warfare, irregular warfare and cyber warfare with other influencing methods such as fake news, diplomacy and foreign electoral intervention. It's a major wake-up call. Countries will try to resort to rejigging of interest rates & taxes and issue bonds to mitigate economic woos. In the coming days, we can expect:

- Increase in money laundering

- More unemployment

- Increase in crime rates

India has given a lesson to the World. She has shown to the world the difference between governance and leadership. Indian people have rallied around the Government on Covid-19. When people deliver something unprecedented, they'll raise the bar for themselves. Once people's view of what is possible is expanded, they can act creatively and deliver in any situation. Competencies that lead to breakthrough performance are acquired by practice and immersion. The recognition of current limits affords a measure of choice in stepping beyond those limits. Once you have achieved results that first seemed impossible, you can't sit back.

High rate of infection could be the number of "touches" a New Yorker goes through in a day – from the door handle to elevator buttons to the mailbox to subway turnstiles to vending machines to the inevitable handshakes, it is one long touchy-feely day. Anthony Fauci, the infectious diseases pundit and Man-Friday to President Trump in the U.S, recommends people abjure all unnecessary physical contact; leaders of a Western society that signed off till recently with "hugs and kisses" are suddenly embracing the Indian Namaste and the Japanese Ojigi (bowing). Now, every World Leader avoids hugging and hand-shaking; they realize, Indian way of greeting, "Namaste" is safer.

To recall words of great Indian personalities:

Sant Tulsidas (1532 –1623) Hindu Vaishnava saint and poet, renowned for his devotion to the deity Rama:

Faith is that which dispels desire, Devotion is that which generates knowledge. And Vedas say that knowledge is that which fashions freedom.

In 'dependence' there is no happiness even in a dream

Swami Vivekananda (Indian philosopher):

Civilizations have arisen in other parts of the world. In ancient and modern times, wonderful ideas have been carried forward from one race to another... But mark you, my friends, it has always been with the blast of war trumpets and the march of embattled cohorts. Each idea had to be soaked in a deluge of blood..... Each word of power had to be followed by the groans of millions, by the wails of orphans, by the tears of widows. This, many other nations have taught; but India for thousands of years peacefully existed. Here activity prevailed when even Greece did not exist... Even earlier, when history has no record, and tradition dares not peer into the gloom of that intense past, even from until now, ideas after ideas have marched out from her, but every word has been spoken with a blessing behind it and peace before it. We, of all nations of the world, have never been a conquering race, and that blessing is on our head, and therefore we live....!

Mahatma Gandhi, India's father of Nation:

I believe that the civilization India has evolved is not to be beaten in the world. Nothing can equal the seeds sown by our ancestry. Rome went; Greece shared the same fate; the might of the Pharaohs was broken; Japan has become westernized; of China nothing can be said; but India is still, somehow or other, sound at the foundation.

Rabindranath Tagore (Indian poet & philosopher):

India has all along been trying experiments in evolving a social unity within which all the different peoples could be held together, while fully enjoying the freedom of maintaining their differences. The tie has been as loose as possible, yet as close as circumstances permitted. This has produced something like the United States of a social federation, whose common name is Hinduism.

To protect the virtuous and re-establish dharma, God takes a human form from age to age. Avatars appear time and again only to help human beings, by leading an exemplary life and demonstrating how to lead a good life. Examples are Sheshadri Swamigal, Ramana Maharshi, Shirdi Sai Baba, Puttaparthi Sathya Sai Baba and Jagadguru Shri Chandrasekharendra Saraswati Swamigal (also known as the Sage of Kanchi and Kanchi Sri Maha Periva). Their teachings are very relevant in everyday life.

Every phase in our life is bound to teach us something valuable; it depends on us whether we understand the lessons or just turn the page.

India is the Country which has imposed the largest lockdown in the history of our Planet – 1.3 billion people! The Serum Institute of India can produce 1.5 billion vaccines a year, much more than any similar institute either in the U.S or China. Besides such large production, it is also at low cost. Oxford has given Serum Institute of India to produce "test vaccines" and production is going on. If the tests are successful, India will also be known as the Country which saved the World. Humanity can win only if all Countries come together.

U.S, U.K, India, Canada, Belgium, Norway, Switzerland, Germany, the Netherlands, Australia, Italy and China are all working on developing a coronavirus vaccine as soon as possible. A Coalition for Epidemic Preparedness Innovations (CEPI) has identified at least 115 ongoing vaccine initiatives worldwide. And the race is shattering norms of speed and safety in drug and vaccine development. It is expected that a vaccine will be ready anywhere from 12 to 18 months from now. "That is a very, very rapid timeline,"

If the invisible virus can scare us then the invisible GOD has the power to save us! Belief creates the path; Bhagavad Gita also says: "do your duty and leave the rest to GOD". When you can't control what's happening, challenge yourself to control the way you respond to what's happening. That's where your power is. We need to keep going through lock-down; difficult roads often lead to beautiful destinations. This is what India is trying to do. With log-down and social distancing, human-beings have the flair to consume constant information; a strong mind can overtake the fear which has already overtaken humanity. The people who make a difference in our life are the ones who care the most and not the ones with the most credentials, the most money...or the most awards.

We don't need to worry about the world coming to an end today. It's already tomorrow in Australia! Cherish what you have. Locked down and social distancing is an opportunity to do what you always wanted to do..

A Philosopher once said "The deepest prison, sealed off from light and sound, cannot hold the human spirit if hope endures." Yes, the entire humanity is under lockdown and prisoned in their respective homes fearing the deadliest virus COVID-19. In this time of despair it is but only the inner spirit of humans that can keep us all in good stead. Human mind and parachute have one thing in common; both are useful, only when they are open. A barge will drift if she has no anchor; by "open" *it is not drifting,* but focused. Now is the time for nations to treat all human-beings as children of GOD, beyond their borders, boundaries, race and aversion. When we die – whether cremated or buried, all life is eventually reunited with the Earth - that we are all part of the same energy. The Stoics of ancient Greece called this sympatheia, the feeling that the universe is an indivisible, unified living organism endlessly in flux.

The World is yet to learn a good lesson from coronavirus. There is debate on which medicine - Remdesivir or Hydroxychloroquine is more effective.

Also, is it pneumonia or disseminated intravascular coagulation (thrombosis)? Lobbyists are having a field-day. *Though research is ongoing to find a vaccination for cure, it is long shot; in all probabilities, corona has come to stay and only way to handle this virus is to strengthen immunity.* ORAC is Oxygen Radical Absorbance Capacity. Higher ORAC, better will be oxygen carrying capacity of blood & in Lungs; like *"Intel inside in computers"*, we have to build immunity inside! In any case Herd immunity is a long shot.

Unfortunately, the virus has hit the U.S when the Presidential election is due later this year, Donald Trump vying for second term. *U.S unemployment toll has hit about 36 million.*

Michael Pillsbury U.S. government's leading China experts reveals in his book, "The Hundred-Year Marathon" published in 2015 the hidden strategy fueling China's rise – and how Americans have been seduced into helping China overtake U.S as the world's leading superpower by 2049, the one-hundredth anniversary of the founding of the People's Republic. It looks as though China is running faster to beat this clock. It is a long walk to get over Covid-19 and requires countries to walk together; if China wants to run fast, let them run alone.

Hindus swim in the holy river Ganges, hoping to get some blessings amidst the floating garbage; with faith, *people avoid the garbage* and swear by the Ganges and continue to swim in it. A good example to the world to deal with China for saving their citizen and economy.

Spiritual Maturity to differentiate between "need" & "want" and able to let go of our wants; stop attaching "happiness" to material things. The world then will change for the better. The Vedic lesson to the World:

- ✦ Lokah Samastah Sukhino Bhavantu
- ✦ Sarve Janah Sukhino Bhavantu

Meaning, "May all be prosperous and happy" and "May the whole world live in happiness". Expanding these further "May all beings everywhere be happy and free, and may the thoughts, words, and actions of my own life contribute in some way to that happiness and to that freedom for all." These mantra moves from our personal self and ego to radiate a prayer of love for the global wellbeing. It is a reminder we are a part of the universe and can positively impact all of creation. Inherent in the mantra is that we are all beings sharing the same planet and we must care equally for other inhabitants. They expand us beyond just the clan or tribe mentality and remind us we are interconnected to all. We all share the same life experiences, of pain and pleasure, loss and enlightenment, love and doubt. We can see the woes of mankind are all shared, independent of time or location. This is the need of the hour to inculcate traditional & cultural values in younger generation.

PICTURES OF PAST PANDEMICS

Thursday, November 7th, 1918

CORPORATION OF THE CITY OF KELOWNA

PUBLIC NOTICE

Notice is hereby given that, in order to prevent the spread of Spanish Influenza, all Schools, public and private, Churches, Theatres, Moving Picture Halls, Pool Rooms and other places of amusement, and Lodge meetings, are to be closed until further notice.

All public gatherings consisting of ten or more are prohibited.

D. W. SUTHERLAND,
Mayor.

Kelowna, B.C.,
19th October, 1918.

QUARANTENA

Persian scholar of medicine, Ibn Sina (980-1037), suspected that some diseases were spread by microorganisms. To prevent human-to-human contamination, he came up with the method of isolating people for 40 days. He called this "al-arba'iniya", the forty.

Traders from Venice heard of his success and took this knowledge back to Italy. They called it "quarantena", the forty in Italian.

This is where the word quarentine comes from.

SAVE YOURSELF

——FROM INFLUENZA AND——

PNEUMONIA	TUBERCULOSIS	WHOOPING COUGH
BAD COLDS	DIPHTHERIA	MENINGITIS
MEASLES	SCARLET FEVER	MUMPS

FOLLOW TWO SIMPLE RULES

RULE 1

Whenever you cough or sneeze, bow your head or put a handkerchief over your mouth and nose.

RULE 2

Don't put in your mouth fingers, pencils, or anything else that does not belong there, nor use a common drinking cup.

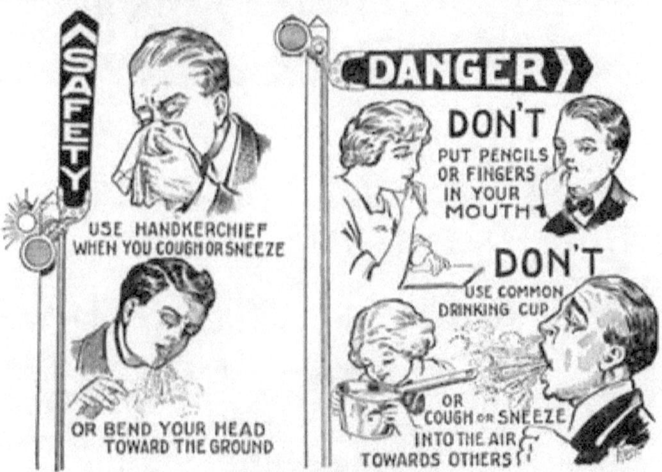

The Germs of these Diseases are spread through the secretions of the mouth and nose of sick people and carriers.

Furnished by THE VIRGINIA STATE BOARD OF HEALTH

PLEASE POST · Council of National Defense, C. R. Keiley, Federal Field Secretary

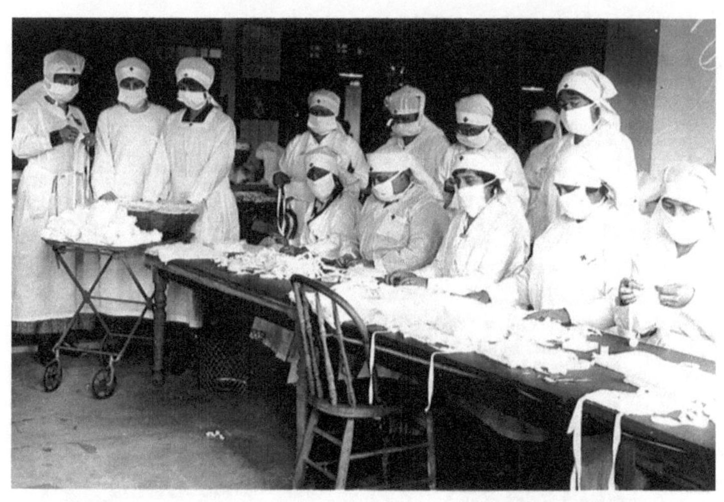

BEMIDJI DAILY PIONEER

PUBLIC PLACES ARE ORDERED CLOSED

GERMANY'S REPLY HANDED TO SWISS MINISTER; KAISER'S ALLIES WOULD QUIT

MAYOR ISSUES ORDER TO PREVENT SPREAD INFLUENZA PLAGUE

DON'T DO THESE THINGS!

Don't kiss your sweetheart while "Spanish flu" or pneumonia plague is on!

You might kill her—or him, by passing a deadly germ along.

Kissing Spreads "Flu"

Don't sneeze or cough in anybody's face. Use your handkerchief to cover nose and mouth.

DO THESE THINGS!

"Spanish flu" is staging a "comeback."

Medical authorities fear it will attack 40 per cent of the people.

Doctors and nurses everywhere are overtaxed in the fight.

They need the help of every person in the community in preventive measures.

In 1962, an Italian magazine did a story about what the world would look like in 2022. Thoughts??

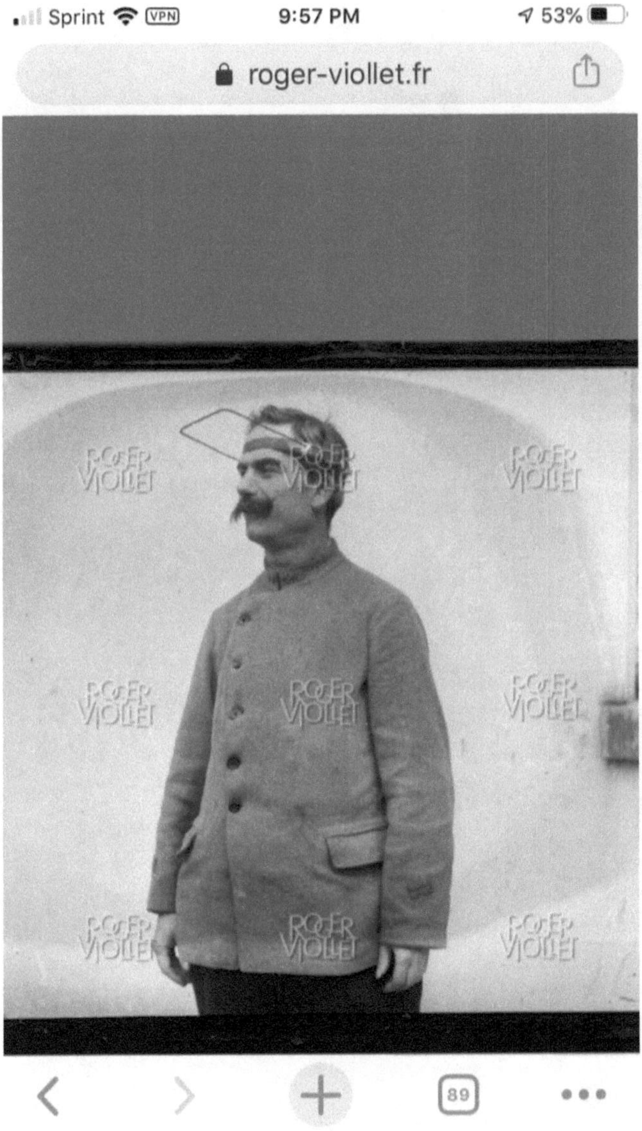
Sprint
VPN
9:57 PM
53%
roger-viollet.fr
ROGER VIOLLET
89

ROGER
VIOLLET
ROGER
VIOLLET
ROGER
VIOLLET

WEAR A MASK
OR GO TO JAIL

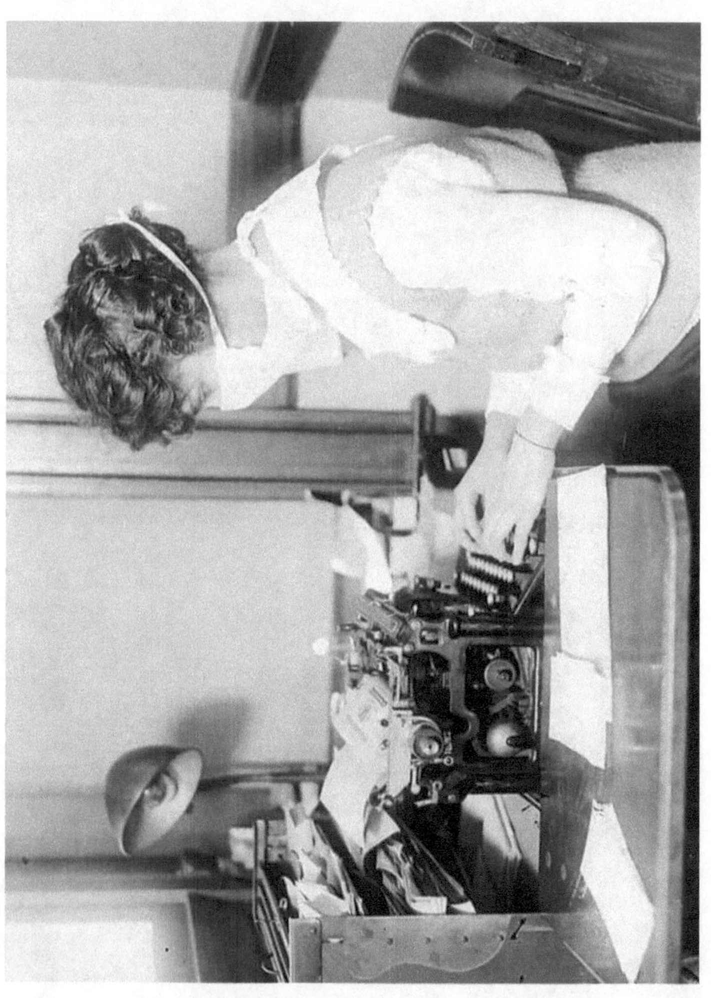

CLOTHES
CHESTY'S
COOPER
SPORTING GOODS
CHESTY'S

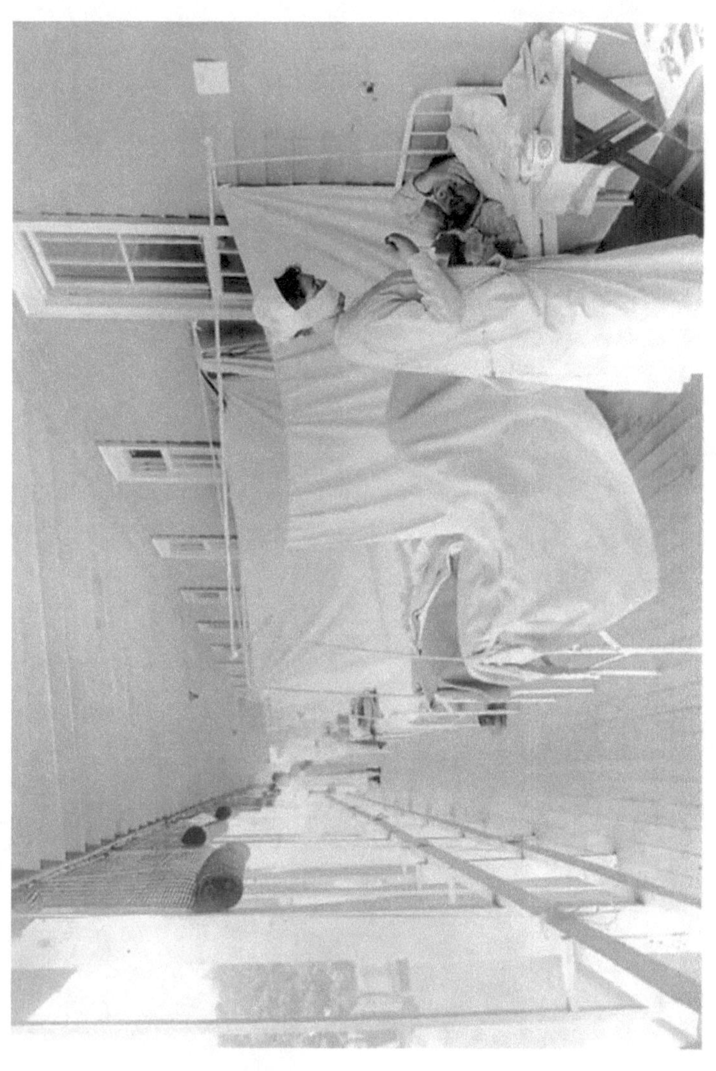